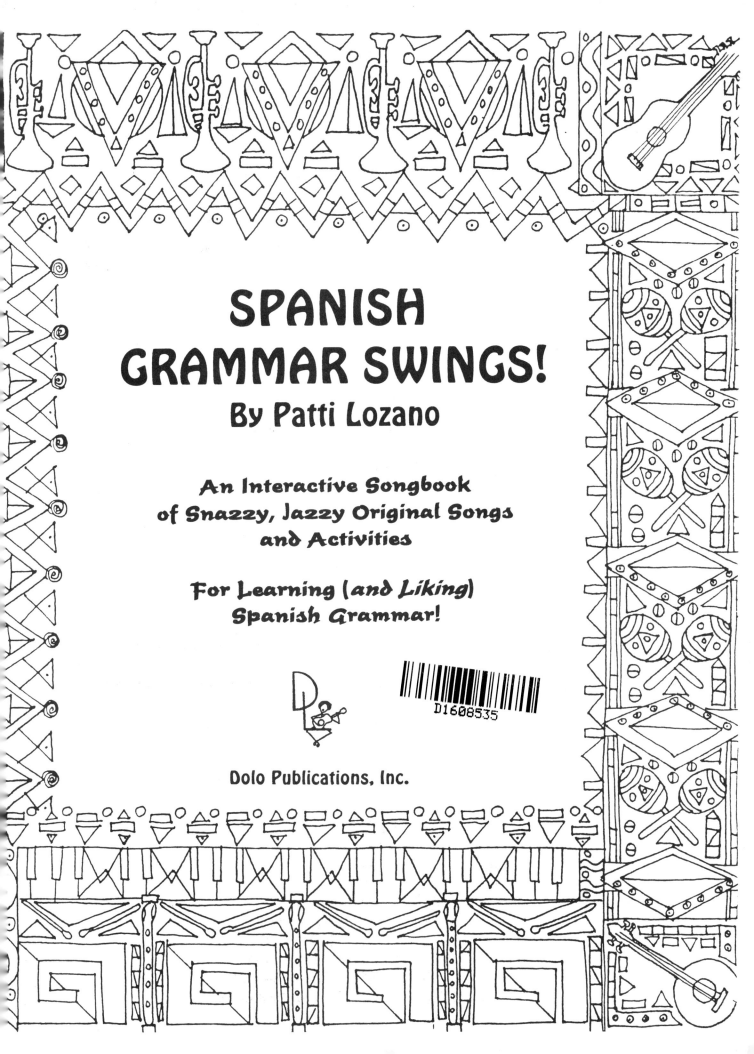

SPANISH GRAMMAR SWINGS!
By Patti Lozano

**An Interactive Songbook
of Snazzy, Jazzy Original Songs
and Activities**

*For Learning (and Liking)
Spanish Grammar!*

Dolo Publications, Inc.

Cover and interior art by Jan Bertoli

Copyright ©Patti Lozano 2001
All Rights Reserved
First Printing 2001
Printed in the United States of America

ISBN 0-9650980-9-5

Dolo Publications, Inc.
12800 Briar Forest Drive #23
Houston, Texas 77077-2201
(281)493-4552 or (281)463-6694
fax: (281)679-9092 or (281)463-4808
e-mail: dolo@wt.net or plozano@swbell.net

Acknowledgments

I am very proud of this new book. Many people contributed their time and talents to make **Spanish Grammar Swings!** a reality. I especially want to thank the following people:

Tina Hill and her Spanish students at Carlos Watkins Middle School — for singing with me, and for giving me so many great ideas for songs and activities.

Alberto, my husband, and Renate Donovan, my mother — for their editing and suggestions, and for tolerating me for the long haul.

Harold Donovan — for the book title

Dr. David Long, and CySprings High School teachers Rosa Bowen and Brenda Bauske — for proofing the final drafts of the manuscript.

Margie Schneider — for brainstorming ideas with me, trying out harmonies and choreography, and for always being there to help when I really need it

Thank you to these musicians for putting the "jazz" and "pizzazz" into my melodies: my friend Jan Caviel and her phenomenal keyboard skills, my friend and banjo player, Frank Miller, and my very talented son and drummer, Ari Lozano.

Thank you also to Northbrook High School choir director, Gabriel Perez, and his gifted singers, Daniela Aguilar, Melissa Durán and Julio César Guerrero for their lovely voices on the recording. Thanks also to Juan Gabriel Pareja for donating his time and considerable singing abilities on the recording.

Finally, a huge thank you to my good friend, Jan Bertoli, for her exquisite "neo Aztec" artwork on the book cover, and her clever illustrations throughout the book.

Other works by Patti Lozano
(Published by Dolo Publications, Inc.)

Music That Teaches Spanish!
More Music That Teaches Spanish!
Leyendas con canciones
Mighty Mini-Plays for the Spanish Classroom
Mighty Mini-Plays for the French Classroom
Mighty Mini-Plays for the German Classroom
Mighty Mini-Plays for the ESL Classroom
Music That Teaches English!
Music That Teaches French!
Music That Teaches German!
Get Them Talking!
Teatro de Cuentos de Hadas

Contents

Introduction

How the songs were born

Spanish Grammar Swings! has been three long years in the making. It's inception came when my son, Ari, began his formal Spanish language instruction in 7th grade. His teacher, Tina Hill, was already using two of my earlier song/activity books, **Music That Teaches Spanish!** And **More Music That Teaches Spanish!**, but her students had no catchy songs to specifically address grammar points. So, in order to help Ms. Hill, as the students were introduced to basic structures in the textbook, I composed songs to reinforce them and to bring them to life. *"La mochila", "¿De dónde eres?", "Yo soy muy tímido" and "No soy nada especial"* were all written for the Spanish students of Carlos Watkins Middle School in the Cypress-Fairbanks Independent School District in Houston, Texas.

I figured that the most important song in the book would be the regular verb conjugation song, because grammar and verbs are the mortar that holds all the rest of language in place. Over the three years, in the shower... the car... in my office... in hotel rooms, I wrote countless melodies and lyrics emphasizing *ar/er/ir* present tense verb conjugation, none of which I liked. The recording of these songs commenced in September 2000; by the end of November fourteen songs were complete, and I still didn't have a "verb" song! The final week of recording, as I loaded my guitar into the car, agonizing as always over the elusive and still non-existent verb song, I heard my son, Ari, play a rolling and pounding "swing" beat on his drum set upstairs. I started conjugating and composing right there in the driveway and minutes later *"Un fuerte aplauso para el verbo 'andar'!"* was born. A friend suggested in passing that I ought to write a song about how overloaded kids are today with homework and extra-curricular activities. I took her up on the idea and fused the *"tener que"* and *"acabar de"* structures with the daily stresses of student life to create the bluegrass song, *"Tienes que trabajar".*

At conferences and workshops I played these songs for teachers, who in turn mentioned additional grammar concepts they wished to see addressed in song. *"A Luis le gusta", "Voy, vas, va, vamos, van"" and "La Palapa"* were composed for them.

Three songs, *"Preguntas y respuestas", "Estoy andando, estoy buscando",* and *"¡Abre tu libro! ¡Ábrelo! ¡Ábrelo!"* were composed after listening to high school Spanish I and II students struggle with question words, the gerund, and commands with direct object pronouns.

"La vida es así" is a song that I composed a decade ago for National Textbook Company's *"¡Viva el español!"* series, and they kindly gave me permission to include it in this volume.

"Tú me regalaste un pastel ayer" is a title that popped into my head when I was searching for a song to highlight the preterite tense. Unfortunately, I had no song to go with the wonderful title. As luck would have it, that week there was a blurb in the newspaper about a dog that swallowed an engagement ring! The song was easy to write after that!

"En el pueblo" was composed for the middle school Spanish students of Appleton, Wisconsin. I was to work with groups of more than five hundred students at a time in an auditorium setting, and I needed an interactive song with a capital "I" to keep them entertained and focused on prepositional phrases. I needed a song with "the works" –

choreography, echoes, cumulative devices, improvisation, drawing activities and an interesting theme. *"En el pueblo"* did the trick; the Appleton students were happy and I was satisfied – and relieved!

Language through music

Teachers have known for years that singing and chanting are the most effective ways to get language skills permanently established in their students' minds. Music has always held a sort of magic power in the learning of language, but until recently, no one has really understood why or how. Within the last decade scientists and researchers have been studying the positive effects that music and rhythm have on the brain, and have been attempting to discover and record why. Noted neurologist and brain researcher Eric Jensen, author of **Joyful Fluency: Brain Compatible Second Language Acquisition** (The Brain Store ©1998) writes of his latest findings regarding the importance of music in the brain's capacity for memory in his recently published book, **Music with the Brain in Mind** (The Brain Store, Inc. ©2000):

> *"There are two ways in which music may enhance the development and maintenance of our brain's memory system: (1) by activating our attentional systems, and; (2) by activating multiple memory pathways. Music does this by increasing our attention to sounds, timing, perception, while embedding emotional content. What we pay attention to is what we're most likely to remember... it activates and strengthens multiple memory systems for both explicit and implicit memory. Retention and recall are improved dramatically."* (page 69)

Brain research by Howard Gardner has determined that all brains posess varying degrees of certain identified intelligences. To date these intelligences include: verbal/linguistic, logical/mathematical, visual/spatial, music/rhythmic, body/kinesthetic, interpersonal, intra-personal and natural. Gardner additionally states that "Of all forms of intelligence, the 'consciousness altering' effect of music and rhythm on the brain is the greatest." (**Multiple Intelligences: The Theory and Practice**, Basic Books, ©1993)

If Gardner's statement is true, then perhaps the reason that music, singing and chanting in rhythm is so supremely beneficial to language learning and retention is because music and chanting alone inherently and actively involve all of the other identified intelligences.

What does all of this mean for language teachers? It means that out of all the activities you do in class, the songs are what will be remembered. Thirty years from now, your students will probably not remember all of the lessons and rules, but chances are they will be able to recall every line of *"La mochila"*!

Why is Spanish Grammar Swings! unique?

The single most important fact about **Spanish Grammar Swings!** is that is makes the mundane but essential task of learning basic Spanish grammar – fun! It accomplishes this through humorous lyrics, themes that are relevant to adolescent life, and peppy, creative and interactive activities, and c atchy melodies performed in a variety of musical styles.

Spanish Grammar Swings! is a comprehensive song and activity book that highlights and reinforces grammar structures commonly introduced to beginning and intermediate Spanish students. Lyrics, translations, vocal scores, grammar notes, activity suggestions and games are are contained within this volume. Basic vocabulary is introduced within the context of the songs, but it is secondary in importance to the grammar concepts.

The fifteen songs are composed and performed on the recording in an assortment of musical styles that include bolero, ballad, Tejano, calypso, blues, bluegrass, swing, polka, 50's rock 'n roll, and Broadway. All of the melodies are original. They are simple and catchy, but not babyish; students will request to sing them again and again throughout the year.

All songs have been field-tested with students and teachers. The song lyrics are always repetitive in order focus on the grammar objective(s). Most songs invite the improvisation of additional verses so that students can experiment and create with new grammar and structural ideas on their own. The lyrics of most songs contain a subtle streak of humor, or a clever twist of the plot line, which is sure to make both teacher and student smile.

The songs address grammatical concepts beginning with the basic definite and indefinite articles, continuing through present and progressive verb conjugations and tenses, adjectives and prepositions, and ending with a comparison of the past and imperfect tense.

Although the songs were composed with beginning and intermediate middle school and high school students in mind, they will interest and delight all language students, regardless of age and level of ability.

Every song has an interactive component in addition to unison singing. Some songs use echoes, some are "partner songs," some employ "ostinato" patterns, some are cumulative songs and some are role-play songs.   The interactive element(s) of each song, as well as any musical terms, are explained and demonstrated in the "c" ("Grammar Objective and Activities") pages.

Teachers will find **Spanish Grammar Swings!** simple and enjoyable to use with the correlated audio-cassette or audio CD. All song and activity pages are designated as blackline masters. In fact the students' lyrics pages and activity templates are printed on one side of the paper only to facilitate duplication. It is recommended that page "c," the illustrated song, be transferred to a transparency to introduce the song and engage in large group acitvities.

The audio-cassette and audio-CD may not be reproduced.

How Spanish Grammar Swings! *is organized*

Spanish Grammar Swings! contains fifteen original songs. Each song has five sections or pages. They are:

  a. **Songs with musical notation, lyrics and guitar chords**
  b. **Lyrics and literal translations**
  c. **Grammar objectives and activities**
  d. **Illustrated song lyrics**
  e. **Vocabulary cards, templates, games and activity pages**

Let's take a look at each section in more detail.

♪ **The "a" page** displays the song in traditional musical notation with guitar chords. This page enables teachers who play the piano, guitar or autoharp to accompany their students. Students who play band instruments would also appreciate a copy of this page. Diagrams of guitar chords and transposition keys are found and explained in the back of the book.

♪ **The "b" page** contains lyrics to all verses and English translations. The English translations are literal and not necessarily singable. Asterisks lead the reader to the bottom of the the page where subtleties and variations of language usage and vocabulary are addressed.

♪ **The "c" page** is the teacher's lesson guide and teaching suggestion portion of the book. The four topics include:

Grammar Objectives: A text box states the purpose, i.e. the grammar objectives of the song. Sometimes examples are given and occasionally targeted vocabulary is listed.

 This song is interactive!   All of the songs have varying built-in interactive components. Drawn from the historical techniques in folk music and oral literature, methods explained and implemented include echoes, partner songs, ostinato patterns, role-play, songs, chants, gestures, choreography, improvisation, call-and-response, body percussion and leader & chorus, illustration and cumulative songs.   Whenever necessary, procedures are explained explained in an easy-to-understand, step-by-step process. Page "e" is sometimes correlated with page "c".

 Grammar Sprinkles: This section is so called because it is not a real grammar lesson, but a "sprinkling" of additional grammar concepts that naturally follow those highlighted in the song. These optional ideas are expressed in the format of activities, drills or games.

 Try this! Several unique games and activities are suggested and explained, with the purpose of extending, exercising and enhancing the grammatical points identified in each song.   The activities are often very creative word and mind games. The activity templates on page"e" are frequently used with these suggestions.

♪ **The "d" page** is the illustrated song page, and is meant for the students. Song lyrics are illustrated, and typed in larger print, so that students and teachers can follow the content of the song by recognizing the vocabulary via drawings. The teacher is encouraged to duplicate this page so that all students have a sheet. If every "c" page in the book is copied, then each student can have a personally illustrated grammar songbook for the school year! Teachers may choose to enlarge this page as a transparency to use as a teaching tool.

♪ **The "e" page** is an activity page that appears with selected songs requiring templates; it contains the games and flash cards needed to play the creative interactive ideas suggested on page "c". Flashcard illustrations are identified in final pages of the book.

Spanish Grammar Swings! was created by Patti Lozano as a natural progression from her successful vocabulary-centered song and activity books: **Music That Teaches Spanish!** and *More* **Music That Teaches Spanish!** to the necessary and sometimes grammar-centered lessons, necessary for a student to become fluent in and to really understand the language. Mrs. Lozano writes with love and compassion for young people who are trying to learn a new language. Her background as an elementary and middle school music teacher and Spanish teacher has given her a thorough understanding of what students like. Now you're ready to go; turn on the CD or audio-cassette, choose a song or grammar objective, and have a great time singing, because **Spanish Grammar Swings!**

Song and Activity Page Organization

a. Songs with musical notation, lyrics
    and guitar chords

b. Lyrics and literal translations

c. Grammar objectives and activities

d. Illustrated songs as teaching aids

e. Vocabulary cards, templates and
    activity pages

1. La mochila

Words and music by Patti Lozano

Estribillo:

¿Por qué? ¿Por qué? ¿Por qué es mi mo - chi - la tan pe - sa - da? No
pue - do le - van - tar - la, ¿por qué? ¿Por qué? ¡A - yú - da - me! Y
di - me por - qué es tan pe - sa - da mi mo - chi - la, ¿Por qué?

Versos:

Es el
2. Son los
3. Es u-na
4. Son u-nos

lá - piz.   Es el cua - der - no.   Es el li - bro.   Es el bo -
lá - pi -ces...
la - piz...
lá - pi -ces...

lí - gra - fo.   Es la re - gla.   Son las ti - je -ras.   Es el le

-ga - jo.   Es la cal - cu - la - do - ra.

1. La mochila

Estribillo:
¿Por qué? ¿Por qué? ¿Por qué
    es* mi mochila tan pesada?
No puedo levantarla. ¿Por qué? ¿Por qué?
¡Ayúdame! Y dime por qué
Es tan pesada mi mochila. ¿Por qué?

1. Es el lápiz.   Es el cuaderno.
   Es el libro.   Es el bolígrafo.
   Es la regla.   Son las tijeras.
   Es el legajo.*   Es la calculadora.

2. Son los lápices.   Son los cuadernos.
   Son los libros.   Son los bolígrafos.
   Son las reglas.   Son las tijeras.
   Son los legajos.   Son las calculadoras.

3. Es un lápiz.   Es un cuaderno.
   Es un libro.   Es un bolígrafo.
   Es una regla.   Unas tijeras.
   Un legajo.   Una calculadora.

4. Unos/unas

Refrain:
Why, why, why
    Is my backpack so heavy?
I can't lift it. Why? Why?
Help me! And tell me why
My backpack is so heavy. Why?

1. *It's the pencil.   It's the notebook.*
   It's the book.   It's the pen.
   It's the ruler.   It's the scissors.
   It's the folder.   It's the calculator.

2. *It's the pencils.   It's the notebooks.*
   It's the books.   It's the pens.
   It's the rulers.   It's the scissors.
   It's the folders.   It's the calculators.

3. *It's a pencil.   It's a notebook.*
   It's a book.   It's a pen.
   It's a ruler.   Some scissors.
   A folder.   A calculator.

4. *They're some pencils…*

♪ Notes ♪

    * Both "*es*" (from the verb "*ser*") and "*está*" (from the verb "*estar*") are correct. "*Es*" means that the backpack is generally heavy all the time, while "*está*" means it is heavy at the moment, but not always.
    * "*El legajo*" is a manila folder or file. "*La carpeta*" is a common name for the bradded folders with pockets used in schools. You can sing either one.

1. La mochila

This song is interactive!

A. Make and distribute to each student a set of the classroom object vocabulary cards on pages **1e** and **1f**. As students listen to the song, they hold up the correct vocabulary card.

B. Stuff a backpack (*"la mochila"*) full of the objects in the song (be sure to include at least two of each item so the "plural" verses can be sung). The class sings the song while the teacher, and later a student, pulls the items out of the backpack as they are mentioned. (You may want to do this activity without the recording, so that the kids can sing more slowly, giving the student with the backpack more time to locate the correct items.)

C. **"La mochila"** is a partner song. This means that it contains two separate melodies that stand equally well alone, but when sung together, create a pleasing harmony. (You may have already noticed that the last two refrains and verses in the recording are performed as a partner song.) Students should always feel comfortable with the song in unison before attempting to sing harmony.

> *Tips for singing a partner song*:
> 1. Sing the song in unison many times.
> 2. Divide the class into two equal groups. Make sure that each group contains some strong singers.
> 3. Group A sings the refrain; when they move on to the verse, Group B begins the refrain. One group is always singing the refrain while the other is singing a verse.
> 4. If students get confused, try standing the students in groups in diagonal corners of the classroom to "sing at each other". There is strength in numbers!

Grammar sprinkles

A. Have the students draw and label additional classroom objects on the backs of their vocabulary cards. Share and discuss the new words. Either in large or small groups, create and sing additional verses using these words.
   1) Create word lists of things that kids carry in their backpacks besides classroom objects, (such as keys, lunches, lipstick, sunglasses, small toys and so on)

2) Add descriptive adjectives after the nouns in the song, for example:

"Es un lápiz amarillo. Es un cuaderno azul.
Es un libro nuevo. Es un bolígrafo roto.
Es una regla larga. Son unas tijeras afiladas.
Es un legajo feo. Es una calculadora pequeña."

B. Teach or reinforce the phrase *"Hay ___ /no hay ____."* by creating additional verses with "opposite" lyrics. The new lyrics might go:

¿Por qué? ¿Por qué? ¿Por qué
es mi mochila tan lijera?
Yo puedo levantarla. ¿Por qué? ¿Por qué?
¡Ayúdame! Y dime por qué
Es tan lijera mi mochila. ¿Por qué?

No hay lápices. No hay cuadernos.
No hay libros. No hay bolígrafos...

Try this!

A. Chant the song instead of singing it.
B. For a vocabulary exercise, as well as a drill on definite and indefinite articles, pull items out of the backpack and have different students identify them.
C. Try the "**Echo Effect**" exercise: a row of four to six students stands in front of the classroom. A desk or table, upon which are scattered various target classroom objects, is placed at one end of the row, next to the "student leader". The leader picks up the object of his choice and states loudly, "*Es el cuaderno.*" He passes the item to the student next to him, who identifies it in a slightly softer voice. The item continues – in rhythm – down the row of students, each student repeating the phrase in an ever-softer voice. The final student speaks in a whisper, puts the object down, and a new object loudly starts its way down the row of students.
D. Add percussion by distributing the classroom objects from the song to students. They tap rhythms on the object(s) only during that item's line in the song.

1. La mochila

Estribillo:
¿Por qué? ¿Por qué? ¿Por qué
        es mi mochila tan pesada?
No puedo levantarla. ¿Por qué? ¿Por qué?
¡Ayúdame! Y dime por qué
Es tan pesada mi mochila. ¿Por qué?

Versos:
1. Es el lápiz.   Es el cuaderno.   Es el libro.   Es el bolígrafo.

Es la regla.   Son las tijeras.   Es el legajo.   Es la calculadora.

 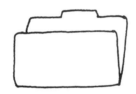 

2. Son los lápices.   Son los cuadernos.   Son los libros.   Son los bolígrafos.

Son las reglas.   Son las tijeras.   Son los legajos.   Son las calculadoras.

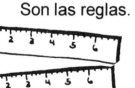  

3. Es un lápiz.   Es un cuaderno.
   Es un libro.   Es un bolígrafo.
   Es una regla.   Unas tijeras.
   Un legajo.   Una calculadora.

4. Son unos lápices.   Unos cuadernos.
   Son unos libros.   Unos bolígrafos.
   Son unas reglas.   Unas tijeras.
   Unos legajos.   Unas calculadoras.

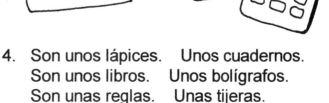

1. La mochila

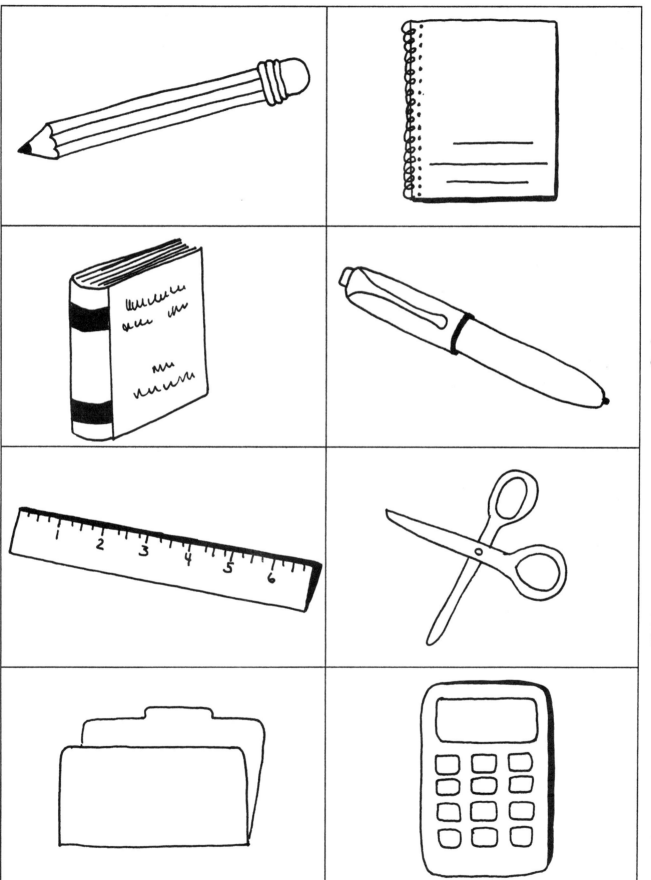

See page 18 for a word list of these illustrations

1. La mochila

See page 18 for a word list of these illustrations

2. ¿De dónde eres?

Words and music by Patti Lozano

¿Có-mo te lla -mas? *(echo)* Me lla-mo Mi -guel. *(echo)* ¿Cuál es tu
¿Có-mo te lla - mas - ? Me lla -mo Ma-ri - lú - . ¿Cuál es tu
¿Có-mo se lla -ma u - sted? Me lla-mo Do -ña Luz - . ¿Cuál es su

nom - bre? *(echo)* Mi nom-bre es Mi - guel. *(echo)* ¿De dón -de
nom - bre - ? Mi nom-bre es Ma-ri - lú - . ¿De dón -de
nom - bre - ? Mi nom-bre es Do - ña Luz - . ¿De dón -de

e - res? *(echo)* Yo soy de E -cua dor. *(echo)* Mucho gus-to (en) co-no
e - res - ? Yo soy de el Pe - rú - . Mu -cho gu-sto co - no
es u- sted - ? Yo soy de El Sal -va -dor - . Mu -cho gu-sto co - no

-cer - te. *(echo)* Es un pla - cer. *(echo)*
-cer - te - . Es un pla - cer - .
-cer - le - . Es un pla - cer - .

2. ¿De dónde eres?

¿Cómo te llamas?

    Me llamo Miguel.

¿Cuál es tu nombre?

    Mi nombre es Miguel.

¿De dónde eres?

    Yo soy de Ecuador.

Mucho gusto (en*) conocerte.

    Es un placer.

2. ¿Cómo te llamas?

    Me llamo Marilú.

¿Cuál es tu nombre?

    Mi nombre es Marilú.

¿De dónde eres?

    Yo soy del* Perú.

Mucho gusto (en) conocerte.

    Es un placer.

3. ¿Cómo se llama usted?

    Me llamo Doña Luz.

¿Cuál es su nombre?

    Mi nombre es Doña Luz.

¿De dónde es usted?

    Yo soy de El Salvador.

Mucho gusto (en) conocerle.

    Es un placer.

What are you called?

    My name is Michael. *

What is your name?

    My name is Michael.

Where are you from?

    I'm from Ecuador.

It's nice to meet you.

    It's a pleasure.

What are you called?

    My name is Marilú.

What is your name?

    My name is Marilú.

Where are you from?

    I'm from Peru.

It's nice to meet you.

    It's a pleasure.

What are you called?

    My name is Doña Luz.

What is your name?

    My name is Doña Luz.

Where are you from?

    I'm from El Salvador.

It's nice to meet you.

    It's a pleasure.

♪ Notes ♪

    * Both *"Mucho gusto conocerte"* and *"Mucho gusto en conocerte"* are correct. Often the response is shortened to simply *"Mucho gusto"*.

    * *"Me llamo..."* literally translates to *"I am called..."*

    * Most names of countries do not require the definite article (*el* or *la*), for example: *México, Colombia, Chile, Alemania, Inglaterra.* Some countries do require the definite articles, most notably *el Perú, la Argentina, el Brasil, el Uruguay, el Paraguay, el Canadá, la República Dominicana* and *el Japón.*

2. ¿De dónde eres?

> **Grammar Objectives:** ➤ basic introductions
>
> Examples: *¿Cómo te llamas? ¿Cuál es tu/su nombre?*
> *Mi nombre es _____."*
> *¿De dónde eres? ¿De dónde es usted?*
> *Yo soy de/del ____.*
> *Mucho gusto (en) conocerte/le.*
> *Es un placer.*

This song is interactive!

A. "**¿De dónde eres?**", as you can hear on the recording, is an echo song. Follow these teaching suggestions:
   1) The students listen to you sing it or to the recording.
   2) The students sing in unison with you and the recording.
   3) Divide the class in half. The song lends itself to a "boys-on-one-side and girls-on-the-other" formation.
   4) Divide each half into quarters again. Decide which quarter of each group will sing the "lead" voice and which quarter will sing the echo.
   5) Sing it!

B. Now let's improvise! Choose an eager student from each half to be the lead soloist, i.e. to sing his or her own name in place of "*Miguel*" and "*Marilú*". The lead student also chooses the country that he/she is from. The rest of the students in the two groups provide the echoes.

C. Choose the name of a famous person to be the character, and sing about the country that he or she is from.

Grammar sprinkles

Make a transparency of page **2e**. Place a marker on the person and the country to be the subjects of the song. Singing in either groups or in solos, the students must choose the appropriate grammar form (formal or informal) to address the chosen character. (The dog, who, tragically, does not speak Spanish *or* English, must bark or howl his lines, and his class will naturally echo him.)

Try this!

A. Create enough sets of page **2e** so that each student has one character card and one country. After students name their character and identify their country, they meet in pairs. Pairs share their cards and then sing or chant the song using their card identities. Encourage students to extend the encounter with more phrases they have studied, *i.e. ¿Dónde vives? ¿Cuántos años tienes?*

B. Buy or request from the school nurse a set of wooden tongue depressors. Ask each student to draw a face and torso on their stick, and to name their creation. On the back of the stick, they write the name of a country. Choose pairs of students and sticks to sing or chant the song and to improvise a dialogue.

2. ¿De dónde eres?

¿Cómo te llamas?
    Me llamo Miguel.
¿Cuál es tu nombre?
    Mi nombre es Miguel.

¿De dónde eres?
    Yo soy de Ecuador.
Mucho gusto (en) conocerte.
    Es un placer.

2. ¿Cómo te llamas?
    Me llamo Marilú.
¿Cuál es tu nombre?
    Mi nombre es Marilú.

¿De dónde eres?
    Yo soy del Perú.
Mucho gusto (en) conocerte.
    Es un placer.

3. ¿Cómo se llama usted?
    Me llamo Doña Luz.
¿Cuál es su nombre?
    Mi nombre es Doña Luz.

¿De dónde es usted?
    Yo soy de El Salvador.
Mucho gusto (en) conocerle.
    Es un placer.

2d

2. ¿De dónde eres?

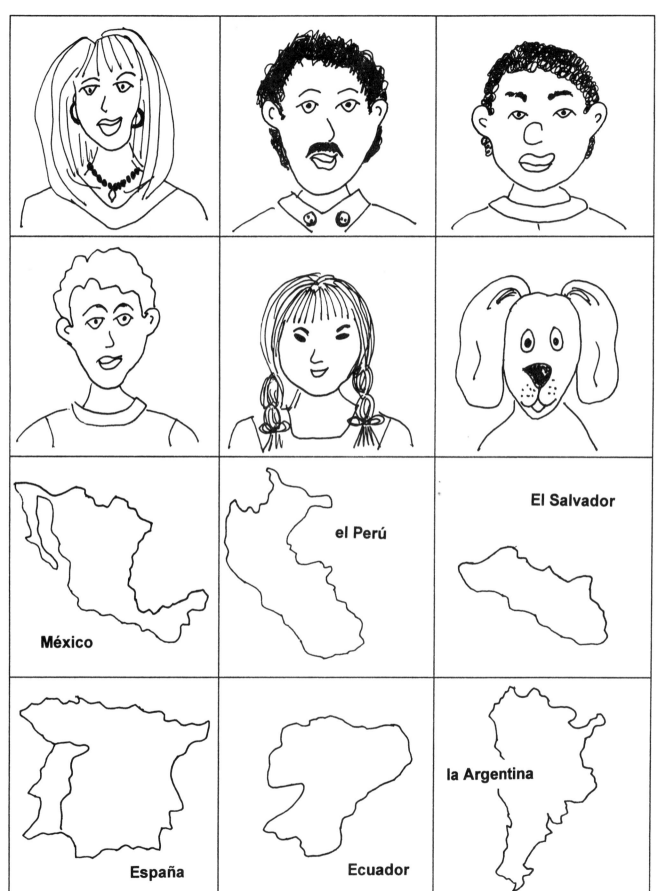

el Perú

El Salvador

México

España   Ecuador   la Argentina

See page 18 for a word list of these illustrations

3. Yo soy muy tímido y por eso no estoy contigo

Words and music by Patti Lozano

Verso:

Yo soy mu - y tí - mi - do y por e - so no es-toy con -
2. Tú e -res muy ro - mán - ti - co...
3. Él es mu - y - cí - ni - co...

ti - go, Yo soy mu - y tí - mi - do y por

Estribillo:

e - so no es-toy con - ti - go. Yo soy, tú e -res,

él es, e - lla es, us - ted es, no - so -tros so -mos,

e - llos son, us - te -des tam - bi - én

3. Yo soy muy tímido y por eso no estoy contigo

Yo soy muy tímido
    y por eso no estoy contigo
Yo soy muy tímido
    y por eso no estoy contigo

I'm very timid
    and that's why I'm not with you
I'm very timid
    and that's why I'm not with you

Estribillo:
Yo soy, tú eres, él es,
Ella es, usted es
Nosotros somos, ellos son
Ustedes también

Refrain:
I am, you are, he is,
She is, you [formal] are
We are, they are
You [plural] are too

2. Tú eres muy romántico
    y por eso no estás conmigo

2. *You are very romantic*
    and that's why you're not with me

3. Él es muy cínico
    y por eso no está con ella

3. *He is very cynical*
    and that's why he's not with her

4. Nosotros somos muy simpáticos
    y por eso no estamos con ustedes

4. *We are very nice*
    and that's why we're not with you [plural]

5. Todos están cansados ya
    de esta tonta canción

5. *Everyone is very tired now*
    of this silly song

♪ Notes ♪

Here is an additional verse that I wrote for this song but decided not to put on the recording. You may want to sing it with your students. It fits the best after verse #4.

Nosotros somos muy elegantes
    y por eso no estamos con ellos

We are very elegant
    and that's why we're not with them

3. Yo soy muy tímido y por eso no estoy contigo

Grammar Objectives: ➢ the verbs *ser* and *estar*, usage and conjugation
➢ subject pronouns (*yo, tú, él... etc.*)
➢ adjectives: number and gender agreement

This song is interactive!

Broadway, here we come! After learning to sing "**Yo soy muy tímido y por eso no estoy contigo**", the students will love to add the following choreography:

Formation: four students in a square, facing each other (like square
  dancers without partners), sunglasses are optional
1) *Introduction*: snap with the recording and look "cool"
2) *Verses*: do the "box" step (instructions follow!) in four beats (You will
  complete the entire box step four times in each verse).
  The "box" step (begin standing with feet together)
      Beat #1: L foot - one step forward
      Beat #2: R foot - one step to R
      Beat #3: L foot - one step diagonally behind R foot
      Beat #4: L foot - one step crossing in front of R
  Once you and your students have mastered the box step, add finger
  snaps on beats #2 and 4.
3) *Refrain*: each student looks across the square at the student facing him,
  and everyone does the "conjugation choreography" as follows:
      "*Yo soy*" – point to own self
      "*Tú eres*" – point to "partner" across the square
      "*Él es*" – pull maginary cap visor (sign language for "boy")
      "*Ella es*" – pull imaginary bonnet chin strap along jaw
          (sign language for "girl")
      "*Usted es*" – boys bow to partner, girls curtsy
      "*Nosotros somos*" – all four in square hold hands
      "*Ellos son*" – hitch-hiking sign with both thumbs over both
          shoulders
      "*Ustedes*" – arms straight down, palms open and facing center
          "*también*" - arms up, fingers spread

Grammar sprinkles

A. Page **3e** contains twelve faces (and groups of faces) portraying different emotions.
  Make a transparency of this page and create new verses, stressing correct use of
  the verbs and the adjective endings.

Example: Las señoras son muy chismosas
y por eso no están con el médico"

B. Create *ser/estar* verses regarding inanimate objects, *i.e.* *"El sofá es muy viejo y por eso no está en la sala."*

Try this!

A. Have your students name famous couples, both real and imaginary. Create verses about them.

> *Example: (from the cartoon, "Rocky and Bullwinkle"):*
> *Rocky es muy listo y por eso Bullwinkle está con él*

B. If you have students in your class who are good friends, ask, "*¿Por qué estás con ___?*" Students answer, "*Estoy con ____ porque es ____, _____...*" etc.

C. Have students bring photos from magazines that they can write verses about. Share them with the class.

3. Yo soy muy tímido y por eso no estoy contigo

Versos:
Yo soy muy tímido
    y por eso no estoy contigo
Yo soy muy tímido
    y por eso no estoy contigo

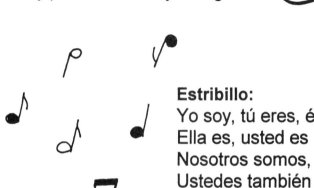

Estribillo:
Yo soy, tú eres, él es,
Ella es, usted es
Nosotros somos, ellos son
Ustedes también

2. Tú eres muy romántico
    y por eso no estás conmigo

3. Él es muy cínico
    y por eso no está con ella

4. Nosotros somos muy simpáticos
    y por eso no estamos con ustedes

5. Todos están cansados ya
    de esta tonta canción

3d

3. Yo soy muy tímido y por eso no estoy contigo

See page 18 for a word list of these illustrations

4. No soy nada especial

Words and music by Patti Lozano

Versos:

1. No soy me-di-a-no, ni gran-de, ni pe-que-ño,
2. No soy in-te-re-san-te, no soy in-te-li-gen-te...
3. No soy gor-do y no soy fla-co...

No soy na-da espe- cial. No, no, y No soy fe-o, ni gua-po, ni bo-ni-to,

No soy na-da es-pe-cial. Y por e-so

Estribillo: Na-di-e me mi-ra nun-ca, Na-di-e me ha-bla nun-ca, Na-di-e me no-ta al pa-sar en el pa-si-llo,

Na-di-e me mi-ra nun-ca, Na-di-e me ha-bla nun-ca, Na-di-e me no-ta al pa-sar en la es-cue-la.

Fine

Chant: Es-cu-cha el la-men-to de mi tris-te can-ci-ón, Es-

pp — *mp*

1. cu-cha el la-men-to de mi tris-te can-ci-ón,

2. Del Capo al Fine   Es- tris-te can-ci-ón!

ff

4. No soy nada especial

No soy mediano, ni grande, ni pequeño,	*I'm not medium [sized], nor big, nor small*
No soy nada especial, No, no y	*I'm nothing special. No, no and*
No soy feo, ni guapo, ni bonito,	*I'm not ugly, nor handsome, nor pretty*
No soy nada especial y por eso	*I'm nothing special. And for that reason*

Estribillo:

Refrain:

Nadie me mira nunca	*Nobody ever looks at me*
Nadie me habla nunca	*Nobody ever talks to me*
Nadie me nota al pasar en el pasillo	*Nobody notices me as I pass by in the hall*
Nadie me mira nunca	*Nobody ever looks at me*
Nadie me habla nunca	*Nobody ever talks to me*
Nadie me nota al pasar en la escuela	*Nobody notices me as I pass by in the school*

2. No soy interesante, no soy inteligente	*2. I'm not interesting, I'm not intelligent*
No soy nada especial, No, no y	*I'm nothing special. No, no and*
No soy calmado, pero sí soy nervioso	*I'm not tranquil, but I am nervous*
No soy muy popular	*I'm not very popular*

Bridge: Escucha el lamento	*Listen to the lament of my sad song*
de mi triste canción (*chanted 4X*)	*(spoken 4 times)*

3. No soy gordo y no soy flaco	*3. I'm not fat and I'm not skinny*
No soy nada especial	*I'm nothing special. No, no and*
No soy débil, no soy musculoso	*I'm not weak , I'm not muscular*
No soy nada especial	*I'm nothing special.*

♪ Notes ♪

You may want your students to sing the adjective endings that are correct for their gender.   In this case, boys will sing the generic lyrics as they are written above, but girls will use the feminine endings, for example (taken from the first verse):

"No soy mediana, ni grande, ni pequeña...
No soy fea, ni guapa, ni bonita..."

4. No soy nada especial

> **Grammar Objectives:** ➢ double negatives
> ➢ frequency words (*nunca, siempre, a veces*)
> ➢ personal descriptions (adjectives)

This song is interactive!

A. **"No soy nada especial"** is an especially effective song when performed with hand and facial gestures to pantomime the meaning of the words as they are sung. You may choose gestures before class or brainstorm them together with your students.

B. You may consider introducing the song via gestures. Students watch closely as you gesture each line of the song, and then pause so that they can write down their ideas.

> *Example: "No" - shake head and wag index finger*
> *"soy" - point to self*
> *"mediano" - palm of hand shows medium height*

Write out the students' compiled and completed version on the board and then compare it to the published lyrics.

Grammar sprinkles

Do the lyrics to this song depress you? (This song is actually one of those most often requested from students. I think they like the idea of this fictional character suffering even more adolescent angst than they do!) For a balancing effect, and also to exercise frequency words, change the lyrics. The song may be unwaveringly positive:

> *Yo soy mediano, y grande y pequeño*
> *Yo soy muy especial...*
> *Y por eso todo el mundo me mira siempre*
> *Todo el mundo me habla siempre...*

Or, for a creative challenge, you may want to try the song as a mixture of negatives and positives:

> *A veces soy mediano, a veces grande y pequeño*
> *A veces soy algo especial...*
> *Y por eso algunos me miran a veces...*

Try this!

A. Are we feeling silly (or spooky) today? Play "**Ghosties**"!

1) Preparation: Bring five old sheets to class and make a list of personal descriptive adjectives with students. Write each adjective on a slip of paper and place all of them into a bag or container.

2) Activity: Pick five students to each grab a sheet and choose an adjective at random from the container. The rest of the class hides their eyes as the "ghosties" cover themselves with the sheets. Each spirit then assumes the position/actions the adjective invokes, i.e. the student holding

"*deprimido*" hunches over, while "*extrovertido*" jumps around and attempts to greet others, and "*exigente*" stands tall, authoritatively wagging his index finger under the sheet.

3) The rest of the class takes turns to guess which classmate is under each sheet, but only receives points if they can also identify the adjective that "ghost" is portraying.

B. Personal descriptions can be a tricky concept to teach because most people are extremely self-conscious about their appearance, and how they think others perceive them. For this reason, on page **4e**, we have the "blob creatures, a.k.a. "*los bultos*," who bear little resemblance to humans other than to possess remarkably human characteristics. Use the blob creatures to play any number of activities, such as:

1) **¿Cuál falta?** Make a transparency of the page and give students a few minutes to look closely at the illustrations. Then tell them to close their eyes. Cover one picture with a small square of paper, then allow students to open their eyes and look again. Ask, "*¿Cuál falta?*" The student that names the missing picture correctly gets to take the teacher's place and the game continues.

2) **"To Say or Not to Say"** Again, from a transparency, to an item and make a statement. If the statement is correct, the students repeat it. If the statement is incorrect, the students remain silent.

3) Use your transparency for a spirited game of **"Matamoscas"**. Give two students fly swatters and have them stand on each side of the screen. When you name an adjective, the first student to swat the appropriate illustration wins a point. The first student to receive five points (with five you can keep the score of each player on your fingers) wins and is ready to accept a challenger.

4. No soy nada especial *handsome,*

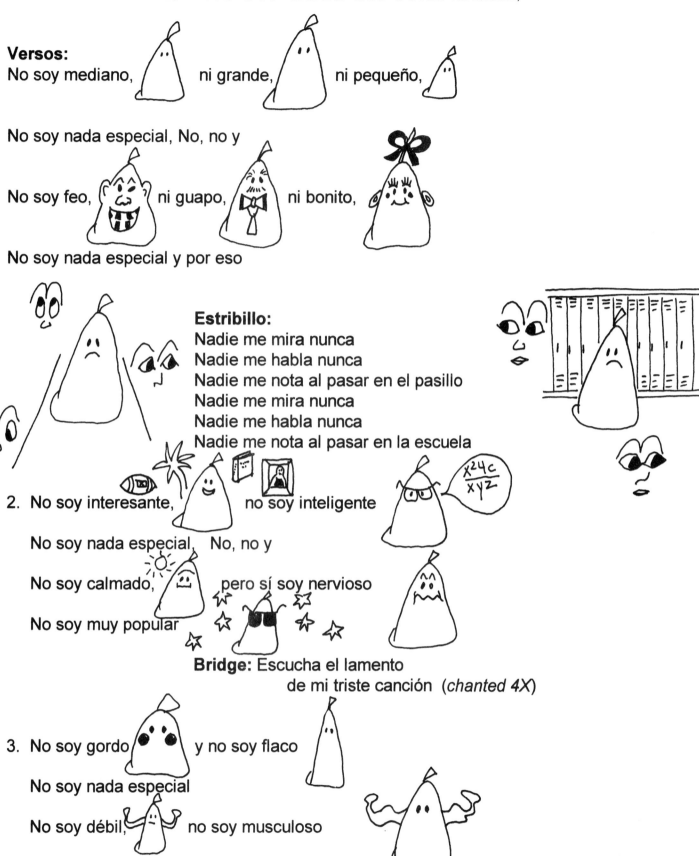

Versos:

No soy mediano,   ni grande,   ni pequeño,

No soy nada especial, No, no y

No soy feo,   ni guapo,   ni bonito,

No soy nada especial y por eso

Estribillo:
Nadie me mira nunca
Nadie me habla nunca
Nadie me nota al pasar en el pasillo
Nadie me mira nunca
Nadie me habla nunca
Nadie me nota al pasar en la escuela

2. No soy interesante,   no soy inteligente

No soy nada especial,   No, no y

No soy calmado,   pero sí soy nervioso

No soy muy popular

Bridge: Escucha el lamento
de mi triste canción *(chanted 4X)*

3. No soy gordo   y no soy flaco

No soy nada especial

No soy débil,   no soy musculoso

No soy nada especial

4d

4. No soy nada especial

See page 18 for a word list of these illustrations

5. ¡Un fuerte aplauso para el verbo "andar"!

Words and music by Patti Lozano

Bolero Style

La fie -sta es qui -e -ta, Na -die quie -re ha -blar Las pa-

la -bras e -stán tris -tes, na -die quie -re bai -lar, Lue -go di -ce el pa -trón, "Ne -ce -si-

ta -mos a -cción. ¡La fie -sta es u -na sie -sta sin el ver -bo, "an -dar"!

spoken: Y ahora, un fuerte aplauso para el verbo "andar"!

2. "co -mer"!
3. "vi -vir"!
4. "tra -ba -jar"!

Swing

(drums) (bass)

Yo an -do, tú an -das, él an -da,

e -lla an -da en el sa -lón, u -sted an -da, Don Ra -món, No-

so -tros an -da -mos, Vo -so -tros an -dáis, U-

ste -des an -dan, 1. E -llos an -dan, E -llas an -dan, No-

2. E -llos an -dan, A -di -ós, an -dar. **Coda** ¡E -llos an -dan, A -di -ós, an -dar!

5a

5. ¡Un fuerte aplauso para el verbo "andar"!

Estribillo:

La fiesta es quieta; nadie quiere hablar
Las palabras están tristes; nadie quiere bailar
Luego dice el patrón, "Necesitamos acción.
¡La fiesta es una siesta sin el verbo "andar"!
Announced:
¡Y ahora – un fuerte aplauso para el verbo "andar"!

Versos:

Yo ando, tú andas, él anda
Ella anda en el salón,
Usted anda, Don Ramón
Nosotros andamos, vosotros andáis,*
Ustedes andan,
Ellos andan, ellas andan
2nd time: Ellos andan; ¡Adiós, andar!

2. comer
   Yo como, tú comes, él come
   Ella come en el salón
   Usted come, Don Ramón
   Nosotros comemos, vosotros coméis,
   Ustedes comen,
   Ellos comen, ellas comen
   2nd time: Ellos comen; ¡Adiós, comer!

3. vivir
   Yo vivo, tú vives, él vive
   Nosotros vivimos, vosotros vivís
   Ustedes viven, ellos viven

4. trabajar

♪ **Notes** ♪

Refrain:

The party is quiet; no one wants to talk
The words are sad; no one wants to dance
Then the host says, "We need some action."
The party is a nap without the verb "to walk"!

And now – a big hand for the verb "to walk"!

Verses:

I walk, you walk, he walks
She walks in the salon (ballroom)
You [formal] walk, Don Ramón
We walk, you [plural - Spain] walk,
You [plural] walk
They walk, they [feminine only] walk
2nd time: *They walk; Goodbye, "walk"!*

2. *to eat*
   I eat, you eat, he eats
   She eats in the salon
   You [formal] eat, Don Ramón
   We walk, you [plural - Spain] eat,
   You [plural] eat
   They eat, they [feminine only] eat
   2nd time: *They eat; Goodbye, "eat"!*

3. *to live*
   [same conjugation pattern]

4. *to work*

* The "*vosotros*" [you plural] form is used primarily in Spain and Argentina. In most other countries, "*ustedes*" serves as the "you plural" form. Some teachers choose to teach it, others not. For this reason I have included one verse with *vosotros* for each ar/er/ir verb. If you don't want your students to bother with *vosotros*, have them clap or snap during that phrase. The final verse, "trabajar", omits the *vosotros* form.

5. ¡Un fuerte aplauso para el verbo "andar"!

> **Grammar Objectives:** ➢ subject pronouns
> ➢ regular *ar/er/ir* verb conjugations

This song is interactive!

A. **"¡Un fuerte aplauso para el verbo "andar"!** is a vehicle for self-expression, once students have learned the song well enough to sing without the recording. (If you're lucky, you have a guitar or keyboard player in your class who can provide accompaniment following the music on page **5a**. Check out the guitar chord page in the back of the book.) When you are not tied to the recording, you can chant the conjugations to any verbs you want, and at your own tempo.

  Choose a different announcer for each verse, who will, at the appropriate time, state loudly and eloquently, *"Y ahora – un fuerte aplauso para el verbo '_____'!"* The announcer chooses the verb and chooses the student(s) to chant the conjugations.

B. IMPORTANT! If you do not teach the *vosotros* form, choreograph body percussion during that line. You can devise simple or complex movements and percussive sounds to fill up those eight *vosotros* beats. Here are some ideas:

Beats: /	/	/	/	/	/	/	/
simple: clap		clap		clap	clap	clap	
average: pat legs		clap		snap	snap	snap	

  You can also let the dance or drill team members in your class come up with some easy choreography to take their minds off the *vosotros* line.

Grammar sprinkles

The kids are going to want to sing this song all year. Make it work for you!

A. Use it to reinforce stem-changing and irregular verb conjugations.

B. Use it to reinforce preterite and imperfect tense verb conjugations. Change the lyrics in the refrain to reflect the tense being reviewed.

  Example: La fiesta estaba quieta, nadie quería hablar
  Las palabras estaban tristes, nadie quería bailar
  Luego decía el patrón, "Necesitamos acción!..."

Try this!

A. Compose different lyrics for the "*Ella anda ___.*" and "*Usted anda ___.*" Rhyming and having fun is more important than having it making sense! Here are examples:

  Ella anda en la cocina   *Ella anda con el tío*
  Usted anda, Doña Angelina   *Usted anda cuando hace frío*

B. To have fun during the mundane but very necessary task of conjugation drills, play "**The Penny Game**":

    1) Preparation: Distribute one penny and 10 markers to each student. The markers may be plastic chips, paper clips, or any small item. Arrange students around the room in small circles of five or six each. Make copies of the verb cards on page **5e**, cut and clip them, and give each group one set to place in the middle of the circle.

    2) Game: Let's say the first verb pictured on the stack of cards is *"andar"*. Student A in each circle taps her penny once on the desk or floor and says "*Yo ando.*" To her left, Student B then taps her penny two times and states, "*Yo ando, tú andas.*" Student C taps the penny three times and repeats *"Yo ando, tú andas, él anda."* Continue around the circle, tapping pennies and conjugating as quickly as possible. When someone taps the wrong number or says the wrong word, that person must put one of his markers in the middle of the circle. When "*andar*" is fully conjugated, place the vocabulary card face down, and begin conjugating the next verb. The circle that finishes conjugating the stack of cards first wins. The person in each circle who has the fewest number of markers left must perform a "forfeit" (see the list of forfeits in the back of this book).

C. Make "**Silly Sentences**" using a class set of the pinwheels on page **5f**.

1) Use these as song lyrics for new verses.

2) Have one student create a silly sentence and act it out for the class. The rest of the class identifies the actions and sets their pinwheels in the correct alignment for that sentence.

5. ¡Un fuerte aplauso para el verbo "andar"!

Estribillo:
La fiesta es quieta; nadie quiere hablar
Las palabras están tristes; nadie quiere bailar
Luego dice el patrón, "Necesitamos acción.
¡La fiesta es una siesta sin el verbo "andar"!

Versos:
(Anunciado): ¡Y ahora – un fuerte aplauso para el verbo "andar"!

Yo ando, tú andas, él anda
Ella anda en el salón,
Usted anda, Don Ramón
Nosotros andamos, vosotros andáis,*
Ustedes andan,
Ellos andan, ellas andan
2nd time: Ellos andan; ¡Adiós, andar!

2. ¡Y ahora – un fuerte aplauso para el verbo "comer"!

Yo como, tú comes, él come
Ella come en el salón
Usted come, Don Ramón
Nosotros comemos, vosotros coméis,
Ustedes comen,
Ellos comen, ellas comen
2nd time: Ellos comen; ¡Adiós, comer!

3. ¡Y ahora – un fuerte aplauso para el verbo "vivir"!

Yo vivo, tú vives, él vive
Ella vive en el salón
Usted vive, Don Ramón
Nosotros vivimos, vosotros vivís
Ustedes viven, ellos viven...

4. ¡Y ahora – un fuerte aplauso para el verbo "trabajar"!

Yo trabajo, tú trabajas, él trabaja
Ella trabaja en el salón
Usted trabaja, Don Ramón
Nosotros trabajamos, ✗ ✗, ✗ ✗ ✗
Ustedes trabajan, ellos trabajan...

5. ¡Un fuerte aplauso para el verbo "andar"!

See page 18 for a word list of these illustrations

5. ¡Un fuerte aplauso para el verbo "andar"!

Instructions:
Place the largest circle on the bottom, the middle circle in the middle, and the smallest on top. Line up the X's. Insert one brad through all three circles. Move the circles around to make Silly Sentences. Example:
"El equipo de fútbol canta en el baño."

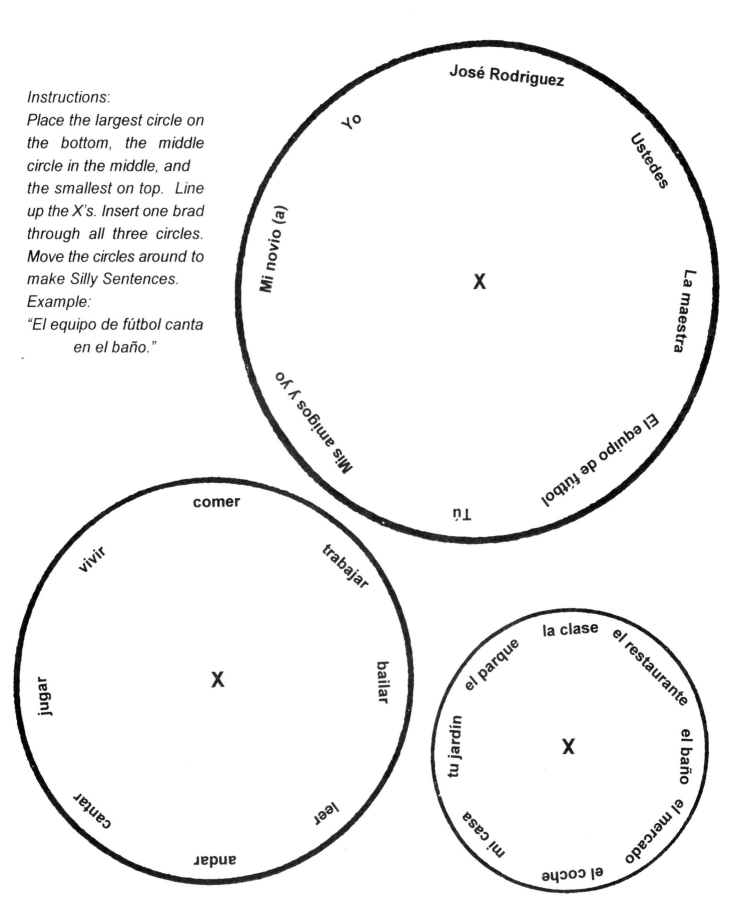

6. Tienes que trabajar

Words and music by Patti Lozano

Bluegrass Style

1. Papá:
2. Maestra:

Es du-ra la vi - da, mi hi-jo, siem-pre tie -nes que tra - ba - jar

Tie - nes que su - frir un po - co, Ten-go que con-fes - ar. Tus her -

ma - nos ya no jue - gan por-que tie-nen que es-tu-di - ar. Es

du - ra la vi - da, mi hi-jo, siem - pre tie -nes que tra - ba - jar.

1. Hijo: A -
2. Alumnos:

ca - bo de la - var la me -sa, a - ca-bo de ba - ñar el pe - rro, a -

ca - bo de lim - piar mi cuar- to, ya quie -ro des-can - sar, Pa-pá. A -

ca - bo de po - ner la me - sa, a - ca-bo de pin - tar la puer - ta,

Ten- go que go - zar la vi - da, Ten- go o - cho a - ños.

6a

6. Tienes que trabajar

1. Papá:

Es dura la vida, mi hijo,
    siempre tienes que trabajar
Tienes que sufrir un poco,
    tengo que confesar
Tus hermanos ya no juegan
    porque tienen que estudiar
Es dura la vida, mi hijo,
    siempre tienes que trabajar

Niño:

Acabo de lavar la mesa,
    acabo de bañar el perro
Acabo de limpiar mi cuarto,
    ya quiero descansar, Papá
Acabo de poner la mesa,
    acabo de pintar la puerta
Tengo que gozar la vida –
    tengo ocho años.

2. Maestra:

Es dura la vida, alummnos, siempre tienen que trabajar
Tienen que sufrir un poco, tengo que confesar
Sus hermanos ya no juegan porque tienen que estudiar
Es dura la vida, alumnos, siempre tienen que trabajar

Alumnos:

Acabamos de leer el cuento,
    acabamos de buscar detalles
Acabamos de contar el poema,
    ya queremos descansar, Maestra
Acabamos de decir los verbos,
    acabamos de cantar los verses
Tenemos que gozar la vida –
    Tenemos quince años

3. Maestra:

Es dura la vida, amigos, siempre tienen que trabajar
Tienen que sufrir un poco, tengo que confesar
Sus compañeros ya no juegan porque quieren progresar
Es dura la vida, amigos, siempre tienen que trabajar

---

1. Father:

Life is hard, my son,
    you always have to work
You have to suffer a little,
    I have to confess
Your brothers don't play anymore
    because they have to study
Life is hard, my son,
    you always have to work

Child:

I just washed the table,
    I just bathed the dog
I just cleaned my room,
    now I want to rest, Daddy
I just set the table
    I just painted the door
I have to enjoy life –
    I'm only eight years old.

2. Teacher:

*[same lyrics as first verse, except
for "alumnos" = students and
sus" = your (plural)]*

Students:

We just read the story,
    We just searched for details
We just recited the poem,
    We want to rest now, Teacher
We just said the verbs,
    We just sang the verses
We have to enjoy life –
    We're only fifteen years old

3. Teacher:

*[same lyrics as second verse, except
for 3rd line: "Your friends don't play
anymore because they want to
progress (get ahead)]*

6. Tienes que trabajar

Grammar Objectives: ➤ tener que + infinitive
➤ acabar de + infinitive

This song is interactive!

A. **"Tienes que trabajar"** was composed with role-playing in mind. Here are some ideas to try:
1) Before listening to the song, read the lyrics to the students. Choose extroverted and knowledgeable students to act out each verse. The roles include:
   1st. verse: one stern father, one son or daughter
   2nd verse: one teacher, several students
   Consider giving minor disguises to actors. Nothing makes students happier than to watch their friends perform in disguise. For example, in the first verse, "father" can wear a mustache and his "child" can sport a beanie.
2) When the song is well-learned, pair all students. All students sing while acting out verses and chorus roles. Note that the challenging roles are those of child/students because of the many verbs they must interpret quickly.

Grammar sprinkles

Often in Spanish textbooks, the structure *"ir a + infinitive"* is introduced at the same time as *"tener que..."* and *"acabar de..."* Either in a large group or several small groups, compose some additional verses using *"ir a + infinitive."* Three-syllable verbs fit especially well into the rhythm of this melody, for example:
   "Voy a escribir la carta,   voy a cocinar la cena,
   Voy a manejar al banco, ya quiero descansar..."

Try this!

A. Create additional verses for the working population, for example:
   * the grocery store manager and the teenager working there
      "Acabo de contar las piñas, acabo de barrer el piso..."
   * the fast food manager and the employee
      "Acabo de cortar la lechuga, acabo de freír las papas..."
B. Play **"What Am I Doing With It?"**
   1) Preparation: Gather several everyday items in a box set in the front of the classroom, (i.e. a plate, pen, CD, cup, paper bag, toothpick)
   Designate hand signals for each structure, (i.e. *"tener que"* - wagging index finger, *"acabar de"* - wiping hands, *"ir a"* - fingers walking)
   2) Activity: Pick a student to choose one of the objects from the box. The student takes a moment to decide either what he has just done with that item (*"Acabo de ____"*), what he has to do with it (*"Tengo que ____"*),

or what he is going to do with it (*"Voy a _____"*). Each item may conjure up several sentences. For example, the plate may bring to mind:

"Acabo de comer el desayuno/el almuerzo/la cena.".
"Acabo de comer en un restaurante."
"Acabo de lavar los platos."
"Acabo de secar los platos."

The student writes the sentence on a piece of paper that the rest of the class may not see. Then he performs the designated hand signal so that classmates can identify the structure. Finally, the student pantomimes his sentence with the chosen object.

3) The class takes turns trying to determine the sentence written on the piece of paper. When the sentence is stated correctly, the piece of paper is shown to the class.

4) The student who accurately guessed the sentence now takes a turn with a different object of choice.

6. Tienes que trabajar

1. Papá:
Es dura la vida, mi hijo, siempre tienes que trabajar
Tienes que sufrir un poco, tengo que confesar
Tus hermanos ya no juegan porque tienen que estudiar
Es dura la vida, mi hijo, siempre tienes que trabajar

Niño:
Acabo de lavar la mesa,
     acabo de bañar el perro
Acabo de limpiar mi cuarto,
     ya quiero descansar, Papá
Acabo de poner la mesa,
     acabo de pintar la puerta
Tengo que gozar la vida –
     tengo ocho años.

2. Maestra:
Es dura la vida, alummnos, siempre tienen que trabajar
Tienen que sufrir un poco, tengo que confesar
Sus hermanos ya no juegan porque tienen que estudiar
Es dura la vida, alumnos, siempre tienen que trabajar

Alumnos:
Acabamos de leer el cuento,
     acabamos de buscar detalles
Acabamos de contar el poema,
     ya queremos descansar, Maestra
Acabamos de decir los verbos,
     acabamos de cantar los verses
Tenemos que gozar la vida –
     Tenemos quince años

3. Maestra:
Es dura la vida, amigos, siempre tienen que trabajar
Tienen que sufrir un poco, tengo que confesar
Sus compañeros ya no juegan porque quieren progresar
Es dura la vida, amigos, siempre tienen que trabajar

7. A Luis le gusta

Words and music by Patti Lozano

Calypso Style

1. A Luis le gus-ta la pri-ma-ve-ra, A mí me gus-ta tam-bi-én, A
2. A Luis le gus-tan las pa-lo-mi-tas, A mí me gus-tan tam-bi-én, A

Luis le gus-ta ju-gar a-fue-ra, A mí me gus-ta tam-bi-én. Si a
Luis le gus-tan las se-ño-ri-tas, A mí me gus-tan tam-bi-én. Si a

él le gus-ta, a mí me gus-ta. } Luis es mi a-mi-go y to-do es-tá bi-én, Si a
él le gus-tan a mí me gus-tan. } Si a

él le gus-ta, a mí me gus-ta } Luis es mi a-mi-go y to-do es-tá bi-én.
él le gus-tan a mí me gus-tan. }

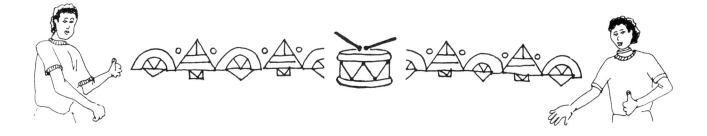

7a

7. A Luis le gusta

1. A Luis le gusta la primavera, a mí me gusta también
   A Luis le gusta jugar afuera, a mí me gusta también
   [Si a él le gusta, a mí me gusta;
   Luis es mi amigo y todo está bien] (2X)

   1. *Luis likes springtime, I like it also*
      Luis likes to play outside, I like to also
      [If he likes it, I like it;
      Luis is my friend and
      *   everything's fine] (2X)*

2. A Luis le gustan las palomitas, a mí me gustan también
   A Luis le gustan las señoritas, a mí me gustan también
   [Si a él le gustan, a mí me gustan;
   Luis es mi amigo y todo está bien] (2X)

   2. *Luis likes popcorn, I like it also*
      Luis likes the ladies, I like them also
      If he likes them, I like them;
      [Luis is my friend and
      *   everything's fine] (2X)*

3. A Luis le gusta dormir tarde, a mí me gusta también
   A Luis le gusta el chile que arde, a mí me gusta también
   [Si a él le gusta, a mí me gusta;
   Luis es mi amigo y todo está bien] (2X)

   3. *Luis likes to sleep late...*
      Luis likes chiles that burn...
      If he likes them, I like them;
      [Luis is my friend and
      *   everything's fine] (2X)*

4. A Luis no le gusta el color gris,
       tampoco no me gusta. ¿Te gusta a tí?
   A Luis no le gusta escribir con gis,
       tampoco no me gusta. ¿Te gusta a tí?
   [Si a él no le gusta, a mí no me gusta
   Luis es mi amigo y todo está bien] (2X)

   4. *Luis doesn't like the color gray*
      I don't like it either. Do you like it?
      Luis doesn't like to write with chalk
      I don't like it either. Do you like it?
      If he doesn't like it, I don't like it;
      [Luis is my friend and
      *   everything's fine] (2X)*

5. A ustedes les gusta mi amigo Luis,
       a mí me gusta también
   Si a ustedes les gusta mi canción,
       vamos a cantarla otra vez.
   [Si a ustedes les gusta, a mí me gusta
   Y vamos a cantarla otra vez] (2X)

   5. *You all like my friend, Luis*
      *   I like him too*
      If you all like my song
      *   let's sing it again.*
      [If you all like it, I like it
      And let's sing it again.] (2X)

7b

7. A Luis le gusta

Grammar Objectives:	➢ *gustar* with the indirect object pronoun (*me gusta, te gusta, le gusta... etc.*)
	➢ negative and plural structures for *gustar* (*no me gusta, me gustan...etc.*)

This song is interactive!

"**A Luis le gusta**" is a simple and fun calypso song that is even more enjoyable with spirited rhythm instruments. Once students are familiar with the lyrics, add certain instruments to accompany the verses (perhaps the güiro and bongos) and others for the refrains (how about the claves and maracas?). You can buy inexpensive sets of rhythm instruments from a toy store or borrow them from your school's music department. Let your band, orchestra and choir kids create the arrangements.

Grammar sprinkles

A. Create and sing an additional verse that reinforces "*no le gustan*".
B. Create and sing additional verses that reinforce "*les gustan*" and "*no les gustan*".
C. Create verses that focus on "*nos*" (i.e. "*A nosotros nos gusta ir al cine...*").
D. Review or introduce other verbs that function like *gustar* such as *encantar, importar, interesar* and *fascinar*. Create verses for these verbs, for example:
         * A Luis <u>le encanta</u> oler burritos...
         * A Paco <u>le interesa</u> su coche nuevo...
         * A la maestra <u>le importan</u> los idiomas...
         * A nosotros <u>nos fascinan</u> los planetas...

Try this!

A. Play "**Tía Zorina**". This is more of a puzzle than a game. Tell your students about the things that Tía Zorina likes and doesn't like. The items should be related somehow. For example:
     A Tía Zorina le gustan los plátanos, pero no le gustan las cerezas.
     A Tía Zorina le gusta ir al almacén, pero no le gusta ir a la tienda.
     A Tía Zorina le gusta ver la televisión, pero no le gusta ir al cine.
     A Tía Zorina le gusta viajar en avión, pero no le gusta viajar en coche.
     A Tía Zorina le gustan las mamás y los papás, pero no le gustan
         los abuelos.

Did *you* figure it out yet??? Tía Zorina likes only the things written with accents! When a student thinks he has figured out what Tía Zorina does and doesn't like, he does **not** explain the puzzle, but instead asks, "*¿A Tía Zorina le gusta(n)* _____, *pero no le gusta(n)* _____?" As students solve the puzzle, they join in stating the lists of Tía Zorina's likes and dislikes.

B. Play "**¿Qué te gusta más?**" The game is written out on page **7e**.

7. A Luis le gusta

1. A Luis le gusta la primavera,
      a mí me gusta también
   A Luis le gusta jugar afuera,
      a mí me gusta también
   [Si a él le gusta, a mí me gusta;
   Luis es mi amigo y todo está bien] *(2X)*

2. A Luis le gustan las palomitas,
      a mí me gustan también
   A Luis le gustan las señoritas,
      a mí me gustan también
   [Si a él le gustan, a mí me gustan;
   Luis es mi amigo y todo está bien] *(2X)*

3. A Luis le gusta dormir tarde,
      a mí me gusta también
   A Luis le gusta el chile que arde,
      a mí me gusta también
   [Si a él le gusta, a mí me gusta;
   Luis es mi amigo y todo está bien] *(2X)*

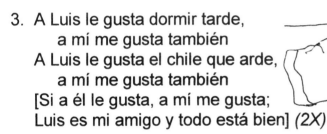

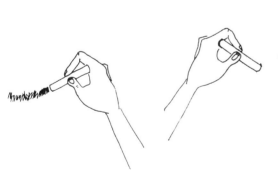

4. A Luis no le gusta el color gris,
      tampoco no me gusta. ¿Te gusta a tí?
   A Luis no le gusta escribir con gis,
      tampoco no me gusta. ¿Te gusta a tí?
   [Si a él no le gusta, a mí no me gusta
   Luis es mi amigo y todo está bien] *(2X)*

5. A ustedes les gusta mi amigo Luis,
      a mí me gusta también
   Si a ustedes les gusta mi canción,
      vamos a cantarla otra vez.
   [Si a ustedes les gusta, a mí me gusta
   Y vamos a cantarla otra vez] *(2X)*

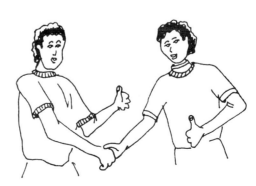

7d

7. A Luis le gusta

¿Qué te gusta más?

Instructions:

1. Write the questions below on index cards (one question per index card)
2. Divide the class into two teams and place the index cards face down in front of the room. Place a pad of blank paper and a pencil next to the stack of cards.
3. The first team member turns over the top card and reads the question silently. The question asks, "*¿Qué te gusta(n) más?*" and then gives two options. The options may both be pleasant – or they may both be very distasteful. The reader decides which option he believes his team will choose, and writes his prognosis down on the pad of paper without anyone seeing it.
4. Now the reader reads the same question aloud for his team. The team may discuss or argue the two options (in the target language,) but they must come to an agreement, voting if necessary.
6. The team states the option they have chosen. If they reader guessed correctly, the team gets a point. Play moves to the other team.
7. The first team to have six points wins.

NOTE: Some questions would sound better using the conditional tense of the verb "*gustar,*" in the question, i.e. "*¿Qué te gustaría más?*" Teach this form if you think your students can handle it.

Opciones

¿Qué te gusta más: viajar en coche o viajar en motocicleta?

¿Qué te gusta más: quebrarte los dos brazos o quebrarte las dos piernas?

¿Qué te gusta más: comer ostiones o comer caracoles?

¿Qué te gustan más: los perros o los gatos?

¿Qué te gusta más: vivir con una persona que nunca se baña o vivir con un ladrón?

¿Qué te gusta más: estar perdido por dos semanas en el mar o en el desierto?

(Hay más opciones al otro lado)

Opciones adicionales

¿Qué te gustan más: las hamburguesas o los tacos?

¿Qué te gusta más: aprender a hablar ruso o aprender a hablar japonés?

¿Qué te gusta más: vivir sin electricidad o sin instalación sanitaria?

¿Qué te gusta más: en una semana escribir dos reportes largos o leer cuatro libros?

¿Qué te gusta más: casarte con alguien guapo y bobo o casarte con alguien feo e inteligente?

¿Qué te gusta más: tener mucho calor o tener mucho frío?

¿Qué te gusta más: no tomar agua en todo el día o tomar agua todo el día sin cesar?

¿Qué te gustaría más: vivir cien años en el pasado o vivir cien años en el futuro?

¿Qué te gusta más: ser viejo y muy rico o ser joven y muy pobre?

¿Qué te gusta más: tener mucho talento pero estar muy deprimido o no tener talento en nada pero estar contento todo el tiempo?

¿Qué te gusta más: pasar las vacaciones en la playa o en las montañas?

¿Qué te gusta más: ir al cine o ver televisión?

¿Qué te gustan más: las casas nuevas y modernas o las casas viejas y románticas?

¿Qué te gusta más: saber patinar o saber tocar la guitarra?

¿Qué te gusta más: esquiar en el agua o esquiar en la nieve?

8. Preguntas y respuestas

Words and music by Patti Lozano

Versos:

Em B7
¿Quién to-ca la puer-ta? Es To-más de la Huer-ta. ¿A dón-de vas? Voy al

Em G D
ci-ne con To-más. ¿Con To-más, el jar-di-ne-ro? Sí, con él por-que lo quie-ro.

F Em D
¿Cuán-do vol-ver-ás? No sé, qui-zás ja-más. Son pre-gun-tas y res-

C G Estribillo:
pues-tas pri-va-das en-tre la fa-mi-lia. ¿Con

C F# B7 Em
quién? ¿Por qué? ¿A dón-de? ¿Cuán-do?

C F# Em Am B7
¿Cuán-to? ¿Cuán-tos? ¿Có-mo? ¿Cuál? ¿Qué? ¡Rá-pi-do! ¿Con

C F# B7 Em
quién? ¿Por-qué? ¿A dón-de? ¿Cuán-do? ¿Cuán-to? ¿Cuán-tos? ¿Có-mo? ¿Cuál? ¿Qué? Pre-

C F# Em Am B7
gun-tas e-ter-nas, ¡no im-por-ta cuál pa-íz!

Coda: Repeat refrain faster and faster
until it becomes impossible to sing!

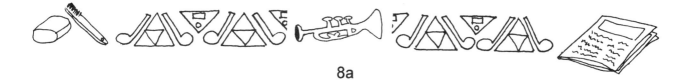

8a

8. Preguntas y respuestas

¿Quién toca la puerta?
      Es Tomás de la Huerta.
¿A dónde vas?
      Voy al cine con Tomás.
Con Tomás, el jardinero?
      Sí, con él porque lo quiero.
¿Cuándo volverás?
      No sé, quizás jamás.
Son preguntas y respuestas
Privadas entre la familia

ESTRIBILLO:
¿Con quién? ¿Por qué? ¿A dónde? ¿Cuándo?
¿Cuánto? ¿Cuántos? ¿Cómo? ¿Cuál? ¿Qué?
¡Rápido!
¿Con quién? ¿Por qué? ¿A dónde? ¿Cuándo?
¿Cuánto? ¿Cuántos? ¿Cómo? ¿Cuál? ¿Qué?
Preguntas eternas
¡No importa cuál país!

2. ¿Dónde está mi bufanda?
      Pregunta a Yolanda.
  ¿Y dónde está Yolanda?
      ¿Quién sabe dónde anda?
  ¿Por qué llevas mi chaqueta?
      Porque es violeta.
  ¿Qué haces en mi cuarto?
      Yo busco mi zapato.
Son preguntas y respuestas
Privadas entre la familia

3. ¿Cuál jabón es de Arturo?
      El azul, estoy seguro.
  ¿Cuál cepillo es de Juanito?
      Éste aquí, el más chiquito.
  ¿Cómo limpio el espejo?
      Con periódico viejo.
  ¿Cuántas toallas usarás?
      Dos o tres quizás.
Son preguntas y respuestas
Privadas entre la familia

Who is knocking at the door?
      It's Tomás de la Huerta.
Where are you going?
      I'm going to the movies withTomás.
With Tomás, the gardener?
      Yes, with him because I love him.
When will you return?
      I don't know. Maybe never.
These are questions and answers
Private among family members

Refrain:
With whom? Why? To where? When?
How much? [plural] How? Which? What?
Fast!
With whom? Why? To where? When?
How much? [plural] How? Which? What?
Eternal questions
No matter from which country!

2. Where is my scarf?
      Ask Yolanda.
Where is Yolanda?
      Who knows where?
Why are you wearing my jacket?
      Because it's violet.
What are you doing in my room?
      I'm looking for my shoe.
These are questions and answers
Private among family members

3. Which is Arturo's soap?
      The blue one, I'm sure.
Which is Johnny's brush?
      This one here, the littlest one
How do I wash the mirror?
      With old newspaper.
How many towels will you use?
      Two or three maybe.
These are questions and answers
Private among family members

8. Preguntas y respuestas

> **Grammar Objectives:**
> ➤ Question words: *¿Con quién? ¿Por qué? ¿A dónde?*
> *¿Cuándo? ¿Cuánto(s)? ¿Cómo? ¿Cuál? ¿Qué?*
> ➤ Question and answer structures

This song is interactive!

"Preguntas y respuestas" is interactive with a capital "I"! The lyrics were composed with a parent and a typical rebellious teenager in mind. Sing it as such. Students must understand all the lyrics before embarking on any of the following activities:

A. Choose a "parent" and "teen" to solo (sing or chant) each verse. Award a Grammy (page **8e**) to the top duet.

B. Have the class choose different body motions to represent each question word. Body motions are performed faster and faster and students sing the refrain faster and faster! Try these gestures:

Question Word Choreography

¿Con quién?	— Point index finger between yourself and an imaginary person
¿Por qué?	— Arms bent, palms upward in classic "What?" position
¿A dónde?	— Make a visor with your hand, peer into the distance
¿Cuándo?	— Point to your wristwatch
¿Cuánto?	— Thumb and index finger measure "a pinch"
¿Cuántos?	— Hands facing up, ten "counting" fingers displayed
¿Cómo?	— Scratch your head in confusion
¿Cuál?	— Palms out, as if holding an apple in each hand, look back and forth at each as if trying to decide
¿Qué?	— Cup ear with hand as if hard of hearing

C. Chant or sing the question words in the refrain as solos. This will involve nine students, with a tenth to exclaim, "*¡Rápido!*" (We enjoyed performing this technique in the recording.)

Try this!

A. Sing the refrain not only faster and faster, but also louder and louder, having a student bark the command "*¡Más alto!*" or "*Más fuerte!*" Try the refrain ever softer with the command "*¡Más suave!*"

B. Play "**¿Dónde? ¿Con quién" ¿Qué?**" This riotous three-part activity may be played by individual players or in teams.

> Part 1: The player thinks of a place. It can be a famous landmark, a city or a geographical location. He then asks, "*¿Dónde estoy?*" (or the team asks, "*¿Dónde estamos?*") The other students guess until they

identify the location. You may choose to let the player use "*sí/no*" answers, gestures, or drawings to give clues. Once the location is identified, move on to Part 2.

Part 2: The player or team thinks of a famous person who is with you at that place. Ask the others, "*¿Con quién estoy/estamos?*" The others must identify (perhaps with the aid of gestures, yes/no, or drawings, as pre-decided) the identity of that famous person.

Part 3: The player or team now decides what he or she is doing in that place with that famous person, and then asks, "*¿Qué hacemos _____ y yo?*" The rest of the class must discover this information as well.

> *Example:* Player A: *¿Dónde estoy?*
>> Class: *(finally discovers) Estás en el mar Atlántico.*
>> Player A: *¿Con quién estoy en el mar Atlántico?*
>> Class: *(finally discovers) Estás en el mar Atlántico con Cristobal Colón.*
>> Player A: *¿Qué hacemos Cristóbal Colón y yo en el mar Atlántico?*
>> Class: *(finally discovers) Ustedes comen camarones.*

8. Preguntas y respuestas

¿Quién toca la puerta?
    Es Tomás de la Huerta.
¿A dónde vas?
    Voy al cine con Tomás.
Con Tomás, el jardinero?
    Sí, con él porque lo quiero.
¿Cuándo volverás?
    No sé, quizás jamás.
Son preguntas y respuestas
Privadas entre la familia

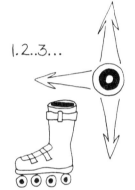

ESTRIBILLO:
¿Con quién? ¿Por qué? ¿A dónde? ¿Cuándo?
¿Cuánto? ¿Cuántos? ¿Cómo? ¿Cuál? ¿Qué?
¡Rápido!
¿Con quién? ¿Por qué? ¿A dónde? ¿Cuándo?
¿Cuánto? ¿Cuántos? ¿Cómo? ¿Cuál? ¿Qué?
Preguntas eternas ¡no importa cuál país!

2. ¿Dónde está mi bufanda?
        Pregunta a Yolanda.
    ¿Y dónde está Yolanda?
            ¿Quién sabe dónde anda?
    ¿Por qué llevas mi chaqueta?
        Porque es violeta.
    ¿Qué haces en mi cuarto?
        Yo busco mi zapato.
    Son preguntas y respuestas
    Privadas entre la familia

3. ¿Cuál jabón es de Arturo?
        El azul, estoy seguro.
    ¿Cuál cepillo es de Juanito?
            Éste aquí, el más chiquito.
    ¿Cómo limpio el espejo?
            Con periódico viejo.
    ¿Cuántas toallas usarás?
            Dos o tres quizás.
    Son preguntas y respuestas
    Privadas entre la familia

9. Estoy andando, estoy buscando

Words and music by Patti Lozano

Honkytonk Style

Es-toy an - dan-do, es-toy bus-can-do en el mer-ca-do a-quí. Ten-go

ga-nas de co-mer pe-pi-nos hoy. Es-toy an - dan-do, es-toy bus-can-do en el mer-

ca-do a-quí. Ten-go ga-nas de co-mer pe-pi-nos hoy.

Y de re-pen-te se me ca-e un fras-co, Y es un gran de-rro-che de pe-

pi-nos en el pi-so. Es-toy an-dan-do, es-toy bus-can-do en el mer-ca-do a-quí. Ten-go

ga-nas de co-mer pe-pi-nos hoy. **Estribillo:** En-tre los pe-pi-nos di-vi-nos y
En-tre los gui-san-tes a-bun-dan-tes

1.

en - tre las ga-lle-tas y pa-le-tas, Tú y yo, tú y yo en-con
en - tre los mon-to-nes de me-lo-nes

2.

-tra-mos el a-mor en-con-tra-mos el a-mor -

9a

9. Estoy andando, estoy buscando

Estoy andando, estoy buscando
 en el mercado aquí
Tengo ganas de comer pepinos hoy (2X)
Y de repente se me cae un frasco,
Es un gran derroche de pepinos en el piso*

I am walking, I am searching
 here in the supermarket
I feel like eating pickles today (2X)
 And suddenly I drop the jar
It's a big waste of pickles on the floor

2. Estás andando, estás buscando
 en el mercado aquí
 Tienes ganas de comer pepinos hoy (2X)
 Y de repente resbalas en el jugo
 De pepinos en el piso, y llegas a mis pies

2. *You are walking, you are searching*
 here in the supermarket
 You feel like eating pickles today (2X)
 And suddenly you slip on the juice
 Of the pickles on the floor and you arrive at my feet

ESTRIBILLO:
 Entre los pepinos divinos y
  entre las galletas y paletas
 Tú y yo, tú y yo encontramos el amor
 Entre los guisantes abundantes y
  entre los montones de melones
 Tú y yo encontramos el amor

Refrain:
Between the divine pickles and
 among the cookies/crackers and popsicles
You and I, you and I find love
Among the abundant peas and
 among the mountains of melons
You and I find love

Estoy ayudándote y secándote
 en el mercado aquí
Tenemos ganas de comer pepinos hoy (2X)
Y de repente me fijo en tus ojos,
Tu perfume de pepinos, ¡Ay, qué fascinación!

3. *I am helping you and drying you off*
 here In the supermarket
We feel like eating pickles today (2X)
And suddenly I look into your eyes
Your pickle perfume, Oh, what fascination!

4. Estamos hablando y riendo
 en el mercado aquí
 Olvidamos de comer pepinos hoy (2X)
 Y de repente yo te doy un beso
 El mundo desaparece, ¡los pepinos también!

4. *We are talking and laughing*
 here in the supermarket
 We forget about eating pickles today (2X)
 And suddenly I give you a kiss
 The world disappears, pickles too!

Estribillo

Refrain

5. Están pasando y sonriendo
 en el mercado aquí
 Tienen ganas de comer pepinos hoy (2X)
 Y de repente salimos del mercado,
 Sin pepinos, con amor y nada más

5. *They are passing and smiling*
 here in the supermarket
 They feel like eating pickles today (2X)
 And suddenly we leave the supermarket
 Without pickles, with love and nothing else

Estribillo

Refrain

♪ **Notes** ♪
 * The first three lines of each verse are repeated at the end of each verse.

9. Estoy andando, estoy buscando

> **Grammar Objectives:**
> ➤ the gerund: (present progressive tense) *-ando/-iendo*
> ➤ present progressive compared to present
> ➤ idiom: *"tener ganas de _____"*

This song is interactive!

"Estoy andando, estoy buscando" is not actually an interactive song. It will, however, keep students' interest because it is a blues-swing ballad (perhaps the first ballad ever to be written about pickles!) A ballad is a song that tells a story; this one is a love story that takes place in a grocery store. Since adolescents enjoy both stories and young romance, this song will surely be a hit with everyone.

Grammar sprinkles

A. There is no third person singular example in this song! Add another character and verse to the story. Perhaps the store manager is unhappy about the romance unfolding in the pickle aisle, hence these lyrics:

> *"Está frunciendo y gritando en el mercado aquí*
> *Tiene ganas de vender pepinos hoy..."*

Perhaps the students have other ideas. Hold a contest and see who can create the best third person singular verse.

B. Work with synonyms. Create totally different lyrics by changing as many words as possible to synonyms. The revisions will probably not fit into the rhythm of the song, so just chant them instead of singing them. The first line might go something like this:

> *"Estoy caminando, estoy mirando en la tienda aquí*
> *Quiero comer pepinos hoy..."*

Try this!

A. Let puppets act out the tender story as students sing it. Teenagers respond to anything quirky. You might try:

    1) traditional plush or plastic puppets, but instead of puppet people, let the lovers be a dinosaur and a rooster, or maybe a cow and a monkey

    2) kitchen tools: as a homework assignment, ask students to each create two puppets out of kitchen utensils; you might end up with a spoon girl and a wire whisk boy, or maybe a spatula girl and a spaghetti server boy

    3) index fingers with whimsical boy and girl faces penned on: this way each student can put on a personal puppet show as the song is sung or the recording is played

B. Have students illustrate a verse of the ballad in each box on page **9e**. Gather the drawings and make transparencies of some of your favorites. Have students retell the story in their own words.

    1) Consider retelling the story in the future tense.

    2) Embellish the basic story with details from the imagination.

9. Estoy andando, estoy buscando

Estoy andando, estoy buscando en el mercado aquí
Tengo ganas de comer pepinos hoy (2X)
Y de repente se me cae un frasco,
Es un gran derroche de pepinos en el piso
Estoy andando, estoy buscando en el mercado aquí
Tengo ganas de comer pepinos hoy

2. Estás andando, estás buscando en el mercado aquí
Tienes ganas de comer pepinos hoy (2X)
Y de repente resbalas en el jugo
De pepinos en el piso, y llegas a mis pies
Estás andando, estás buscando en el mercado aquí
Tienes ganas de comer pepinos hoy

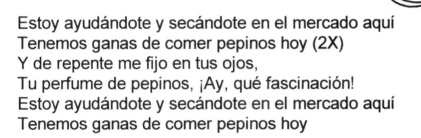

ESTRIBILLO:

Entre los pepinos divinos y
        entre las galletas y paletas
Tú y yo,   tú y yo encontramos el amor
Entre los guisantes abundantes y
        entre los montones de melones
Tú y yo encontramos el amor

Estoy ayudándote y secándote en el mercado aquí
Tenemos ganas de comer pepinos hoy (2X)
Y de repente me fijo en tus ojos,
Tu perfume de pepinos, ¡Ay, qué fascinación!
Estoy ayudándote y secándote en el mercado aquí
Tenemos ganas de comer pepinos hoy

4. Estamos hablando y riendo en el mercado aquí
Olvidamos de comer pepinos hoy (2X)
Y de repente yo te doy un beso
El mundo desaparece, ¡los pepinos también!
Estamos hablando y riendo en el mercado aquí
Olvidamos de comer pepinos hoy

5. Están pasando y sonriendo en el mercado aquí
Tienen ganas de comer pepinos hoy (2X)
Y de repente salimos del mercado,
Sin pepinos, con amor y nada más
Están pasando y sonriendo en el mercado aquí
Tienen ganas de comer pepinos hoy

9. Estoy andando, estoy buscando

10. La vida es así

Patti Lozano

Mamá: Mi - guel, ¿pue-des ba -rrer el pi - so? ¡Pa-ra del so- fá y -

ven- te a -quí! Mi - guel, ¿pue-des ba -rrer el pi - so?

Por fa -vor, a -yú -da-me a mí. *Hija/Hija:* Ma - má, ¡cuán-to quie -ro a -yu -

dar - te! Ba -rrer el pi -so me gus - ta a mí, pe -ro

ten-go que es -tu -diar las ci -en -cias. ¡Lo sien-to pe-ro la vi -da es a - sí!

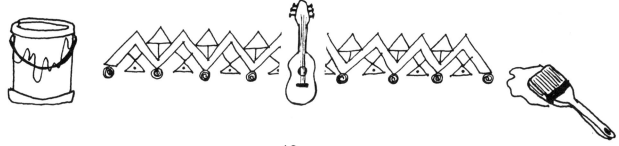

10. La vida es así

Patti Lozano

1. Madre:

Miguel, ¿puedes barrer el piso?
¡Para del sofá y vente aquí!
Miguel, ¿puedes barrer el piso?
Por favor, ayúdame a mí.

Miguel:

Mamá, ¡cuánto quiero ayudarte!
Barrer el piso me gusta a mí
Pero tengo que estudiar las ciencias.
Lo siento, pero la vida es así.

2. Madre:

Inés, ¿puedes planchar la ropa?
¡Para del sillón y vente aquí!
Inés, ¿puedes planchar la ropa?
Por favor, ayúdame a mí.

Inés:

Mamá, ¡cuánto quiero ayudarte!
Planchar la ropa me gusta a mí
Pero tengo que lavarme el pelo.
Lo siento, pero la vida es así.

3. Madre:

Adán, ¿puedes sacar la basura?
¡Para de la cama y vente aquí!
Adán, ¿puedes sacar la basura?
Por favor, ayúdame a mí.

Adán:

Mamá, ¡cuánto quiero ayudarte!
Sacar la basura me gusta a mí
Pero tengo que pintar mi bicicleta.
Lo siento, pero la vida es así.

4. Madre:

Mis hijos, tengo pastel de manzana,
Caliente del horno, lo tengo aquí,
Pero como están tan ocupados,
Todo el pastel es para mí.
¡Lo siento, pero la vida es así!

1. Mother:

Miguel, can you sweep the floor?
Get up from the sofa and come here!
Miguel, can you sweep the floor?
Please help me.

Miguel:

Mother, how much I want to help you!
I really like sweeping the floor
But I have to study science
I'm sorry, but that's life!

2. Mother:

Inés, can you iron the clothes?
Get up from the chair and come here!
Inés, can you iron the clothes?
Please help me.

Inés:

Mother, how much I want to help you!
I really like ironing the clothes
But I have to wash my hair.
I'm sorry, but that's life!

3. Mother:

Adán, can you take out the trash?
Get up from the bed and come here!
Adán, can you take out the trash?
Please help me.

Adán:

Mother, how much I want to help you!
I really like taking out the trash
But I have to paint my bicycle
I'm sorry, but that's life!

4. Mother:

My children, I have an apple cake
Hot from the oven, I have it right here
But seeing as you're all so busy
The whole cake is just for me.
I'm sorry, but that's life!

10. La vida es así

This song is interactive!

"**La vida es así**" is the universal story of sons and daughters finding excuses not to do the household chores their parents request.

A. Divide the class into two groups; one group sings Mamá's lines, the other responds with the offsprings' lines.

B. Develop gestures to illustrate the meaning of the words.

C. Once everyone is comfortable with the song, choose volunteers to solo in each verse and chorus.

D. This is an ideal song for student actors to role-play as it is sung.

Grammar sprinkles

Have students use the premise/plot of the song to write short skits and dialogues. Fleshing out lyrics into more detailed prose will cause students to automatically expand on verb and vocabulary usage. Allow them to practice their dialogues in pairs and present them to the class. Here is a partial example of Verse #1 as a dialogue:

> *Mamá: Miguel, ¿dónde estás?*
> *Miguel: Estoy en la sala.*
> *Mamá: ¿Qué estás haciendo en la sala?*
> *Miguel: Estoy leyendo mi libro de ciencias.*
> *Mamá: Pues, párate, por favor. Levántate del sofá.*
> *Miguel: ¿Por qué, Mamá? Estoy cansado...*
> *Mamá: Tienes que barrer el piso. Ayúdame, por favor... etc.*

Try this!

"**El diccionario dice**" is an excellent activity that develops critical thinking, hones dictionary skills, reinforces target vocabulary, introduces new vocabulary, makes connections, and is tremendous fun!

A. Preparation: You need at least one, but preferably a class set of easy Spanish-English dictionaries, and a list of common kids' chores.

B. Activity: State the chore to the class (*i.e. "Tienes que lavar los platos"*). The dictionary will assist in finding excuses/reasons not to perform that duty. Students close their eyes, open their dictionaries to any page, and place a finger on a word. Then they open their eyes, read the word and definition, and decide how it could be incorporated to make a convincing case for not doing the chore.

C. Choose students to read their words, definitions, and to state their excuses using those words. Who has the funniest excuse? Most reasonable one?

> *Examples: word: banco   No puedo lavar los platos porque voy al banco.*
> *word: batir   No puedo lavar los platos porque tengo que batir un huevo.*

10. La vida es así

1. Madre:

Miguel, ¿puedes barrer el piso?
¡Para del sofá y vente aquí!
Miguel, ¿puedes barrer el piso?
Por favor, ayúdame a mí.

Miguel:

Mamá, ¡cuánto quiero ayudarte!
Barrer el piso me gusta a mí
Pero tengo que estudiar las ciencias.
Lo siento, pero la vida es así.

2. Madre:

Inés, ¿puedes planchar la ropa?
¡Para del sillón y vente aquí!
Inés, ¿puedes planchar la ropa?
Por favor, ayúdame a mí.

Inés:

Mamá, ¡cuánto quiero ayudarte!
Planchar la ropa me gusta a mí
Pero tengo que lavarme el pelo.
Lo siento, pero la vida es así.

3. Madre:

Adán, ¿puedes sacar la basura?
¡Para de la cama y vente aquí!
Adán, ¿puedes sacar la basura?
Por favor, ayúdame a mí.

Adán:

Mamá, ¡cuánto quiero ayudarte!
Sacar la basura me gusta a mí
Pero tengo que pintar mi bicicleta.
Lo siento, pero la vida es así.

4. Madre:

Mis hijos, tengo pastel de manzana,
Caliente del horno, lo tengo aquí,
Pero como están tan ocupados,
Todo el pastel es para mí.
¡Lo siento, pero la vida es así!

11. ¡Abre tu libro! ¡Ábrelo! ¡Ábrelo!

Words and music by Patti Lozano

Waltz (Sweetly)

G / Am⁷ / D / G

La ma - e - stra nu - e - va es mu - y bo - ni - ta. Es
-lá que es - ta cla - se sea fá - cil y di - ver - ti - da. Lu -

Em⁷ / Am⁷ / 1.A⁷ / D⁷

jo - ven y le gu - sta di - bu - jar y can - tar. O - ja -
e - go la ma - e - stra em-

2.A⁷ *retard.......* D⁷ / G Military style

pie - za a ha - blar: "A - bre tu li - bro. ¡A - bre -lo! ¡A -bre -lo!

D / Am⁷

Lee - el cuen - to. ¡Lé - e -lo! ¡Lé e -lo! Bus - ca tu lá -piz. ¡Bús -ca -lo! ¡Bús -ca - lo!

A⁷ / D / D⁷ / G

Mi - ra la pi - za - rra. ¡Mí - ra -la! ¡Mí - ra - la! Con -tes - ta la pre -gun -ta. ¡Con -

G⁷ / C

tés - ta - la! ¡Con -tés -ta - la! Es -cri - be la res -pues - ta ya -

C / A⁷ / G / E⁷ / Am⁷ / D⁷ / G C G

Sién -ta -te, es -cú -cha -me y ¡pon a -ten -ción! Co -rri - ge tu tra -ba -jo. ¡A -ho -ra! ¡Por fa -vor!

11a

11. ¡Abre tu libro! ¡Ábrelo! ¡Ábrelo!

Estribillo:
La maestra nueva es muy bonita
Es joven y le gusta dibujar y cantar
Ojalá que esta clase sea fácil y divertida
Luego la maestra empieza a hablar;

Refrain:
The new teacher is very pretty
She's young and she likes to draw and sing
I hope that this class is easy and fun
And then the teacher begins to talk;

familiar singular affirmative commands

1. ¡Abre tu libro! ¡Ábrelo!   ¡Ábrelo!
   ¡Lee el cuento! ¡Léelo! ¡Léelo!
   ¡Busca tu lápiz! ¡Búscalo! ¡Búscalo!
   ¡Mira la pizarra! ¡Mírala! ¡Mírala!
   ¡Contesta la pregunta! ¡Contéstala! (2X)
   ¡Escribe la respuesta ya!
   ¡Siéntate, escúchame y pon atención!
   ¡Corrige tu trabajo! ¡Ahora! ¡Por favor!

1. *Open your book! Open it! Open it!*
   Read the story! Read it! Read it!
   Look for your pencil! Look for it! Look for it!
   Look at the chalkboard! Look at it! Look at it!
   Answer the question! Answer it! Answer it!
   Write the answer now!
   Sit down, listen to me and pay attention!
   Correct your work! Now! Please!

Estribillo   *Refrain*

plural affirmative commands

2. ¡Abran sus libros! ¡Ábranlos!   ¡Ábranlos!
   ¡Lean el cuento! ¡Léanlo! ¡Léanlo!
   ¡Busquen sus lápices! ¡Búsquenlos! (2X)
   ¡Miren la pizarra! ¡Mírenla! ¡Mírenla!
   ¡Contesten las preguntas! ¡Contéstenlas!
   ¡Escriban las respuestas ya!
   ¡Siéntense, escúchenme y pongan atención!
   ¡Corrijan su trabajo! ¡Ahora! ¡Por favor!

2. *Open your books! Open them! Open them!*
   Read the story! Read it! Read it!
   Look for your pencils! Look for them! Look for them!
   Look at the chalkboard! Look at it! Look at it!
   Answer the questions! Answer them! Answer them!
   Write the answers now!
   Sit down, listen to me and pay attention!
   Correct your work! Now! Please!

Estribillo   *Refrain*

singular negative commands

3. ¡No molestes a María!
   ¡No la molestes! ¡No la molestes!
   ¡No tires el zapato!
   ¡No lo tires! ¡No lo tires!
   ¡No comas ese dulce!
   ¡No lo comas! ¡No lo comas!
   ¡No toques a tu amigo!
   ¡No lo toques! ¡No lo toques!
   ¡No muerdas tu lápiz!
   ¡No lo muerdas! ¡No lo muerdas!
   ¡No levantes la mano otra vez! ¡Otra vez!
   ¡Siéntate, escúchame y pon atención –
   O te mando con el director!

Don't bother María!
Don't bother her! Don't bother her!
Don't throw your shoe!
Don't throw it! Don't throw it!
Don't eat that candy!
Don't eat it! Don't eat it!
Don't touch your friend!
Don't touch him! Don't touch him!
Don't bite your pencil!
Don't bite it! Don't bite it!
Don't raise your hand again!
Sit down, listen to me and pay attention –
Or I'm sending you to the principal!

11. ¡Abre tu libro! ¡Ábrelo! ¡Ábrelo!

Grammar Objectives: ➤ Command forms: familiar affirmative (singular and plural),
negative familiar (singular)
➤ Direct object pronouns

This song is interactive!

"¡Abre tu libro! ¡Ábrelo! ¡Ábrelo!" is a tongue-in-cheek song written about a student's
initial perception of a teacher and class, and how that first impression might rapidly
change. The musical style also drastically changes from a sugary-sweet waltz to
a demanding and unrelenting military march.

A. Stand to sing the song. Sweetly sing the waltz section while gently swaying from
side to side. Sing the "command" section while marching with resolute precision.

B. Divide the class into a small and large group to chant the commands in parts. The
small group chants the *"maestra"* command: *"¡Abre tu libro!"* The larger group of
students are teacher assistants; they chant *"¡Ábrelo! ¡Ábrelo!"* Present the entire
song in this manner.

Grammar sprinkles

A. Conduct a drill that continues building on the above activity. Always trying to stay in
rhythm, the teacher states a verb + direct object command, and the students chant
the appropriate command and direct object pronoun.

> *Example: Teacher: Tira la pelota.*
> *Students: ¡Tírala! ¡Tírala!*

B. Ideas for additional verses:

1) To exercise the affirmative, formal, singular commands, the students give polite
commands to the teacher:

> *Examples: Repita la frase. Por favor, repítala.*
> *Diga la respuesta. Por favor, dígala.*

2) The coaches, music and shop teachers would probably have commands that
differ from classroom teachers. Write verses for them.

Try this!

A. Play "**Simón, the Sly Storyteller, Says**". In this cunning variation, the "*Simón dice*"
commands are cleverly hidden in a story. You may write your own story or use the
one on page **11e**. Students walk in a circle as they listen closely to the story, only
performing the command if Simón says. If Larry, Juana or no one says it, or if
Simón whispers or screams it, they continue walking in the circle.

B. Drill with "**Chain Commands**". Seat students in circles of five to seven. Student A
issues Student B a command (*i.e.* "*Salta cuatro veces*"). Student B executes the
command, then repeats the same command as well as another command to
Student C. Each student in the circle performs all prior commands in the
order they were first issued, and adds an original one. The activity ends with
Student A, who must execute the commands of the entire circle.

11. ¡Abre tu libro! ¡Ábrelo! ¡Ábrelo!

Estribillo:
La maestra nueva es muy bonita
Es joven y le gusta dibujar y cantar
Ojalá que esta clase sea fácil y divertida
Luego la maestra empieza a hablar:

1. ¡Abre tu libro!   ¡Ábrelo!   ¡Ábrelo!
   ¡Lee el cuento!   ¡Léelo! ¡Léelo!
   ¡Busca tu lápiz! ¡Búscalo! ¡Búscalo!
   ¡Mira la pizarra! ¡Mírala! ¡Mírala!
   ¡Contesta la pregunta!   ¡Contéstala! ¡Contéstala!
   ¡Escribe la respuesta ya!
   ¡Siéntate, escúchame y pon atención!
   ¡Corrige tu trabajo!   ¡Ahora! ¡Por favor!

2. ¡Abran sus libros!   ¡Ábranlos!   ¡Ábranlos!
   ¡Lean el cuento!   ¡Léanlo! ¡Léanlo!
   ¡Busquen sus lápices! ¡Búsquenlos! ¡Búsquenlos!
   ¡Miren la pizarra! ¡Mírenla! ¡Mírenla!
   ¡Contesten las preguntas! ¡Contéstenlas! ¡Contéstenlas!
   ¡Escriban las respuestas ya!
   ¡Siéntense, escúchenme y pongan atención!
   ¡Corrijan su trabajo! ¡Ahora!   ¡Por favor!

3. ¡No molestes a María!
        ¡No la molestes! ¡No la molestes!
   ¡No tires el zapato!
        ¡No lo tires!   ¡No lo tires!
   ¡No comas ese dulce!
        ¡No lo comas! ¡No lo comas!
   ¡No toques a tu amigo!
        ¡No lo toques! ¡No lo toques!
   ¡No muerdas tu lápiz!
        ¡No lo muerdas! ¡No lo muerdas!
   ¡No levantes la mano otra vez! ¡Otra vez!
   ¡Siéntate, escúchame y pon atención –
   O te mando con el director!

11. ¡Abre tu libro! ¡Ábrelo! ¡Ábrelo!

Simon, the Sly Storyteller, Says   (Simón, el narrador listo, dice)

Vivimos en un pueblo pequeño.   Nuestro pueblo tiene tres policías. Dos son hombres y una es mujer. La mujer policía se llama Silvana. Los policías se llaman Fernando y Simón.

Cada domingo nos gusta pasear en la plaza. Nos gusta poner la ropa fina y caminar alrededor de la plaza con los amigos. Es como una fiesta. Los policías están en la plaza también.   El problema es que los policías nos piden tanto que es difícil conversar.

Simón dice, "¡Levanten los brazos!" y luego Simón dice, "¡Bajen los brazos!"   "¡Levanten la pierna derecha!" dice Silvana, pero nadie le pone atención.   Luego Simón dice, "¡Bailen!" Nosotros bailamos y bailamos; nos gusta bailar. Simón dice, "¡No bailen!"   Luego el otro policía, Fernando, dice "¡Corran!" Simón dice "¡Corran!" también. Corremos en el círculo alrededor de la plaza. "¡No corran!" dice Silvana, pero nadie le pone atención. Simón dice, "¡No corran!" "¡Salten!" dice Fernando. "¡Salten!" dice Simón. Simón mira nuestras cara y sabe que estamos muy cansados. "No salten!" dice Simón.

Estamos muy cansados ahora. Mi amiga me dice, "Cierra los ojos y siéntate." Pon las manos en las piernas." Luego Simón dice, "Cierren los ojos y siéntense. Pongan las manos en las piernas. Acuéstense."

Descansamos a gusto. Luego Silvana dice, "Abran los ojos y párense! " Fernando dice "Abran los ojos y párense!" No les ponemos atención. Ahora Simón está enojado. Simón grita, "Abran los ojos y párense!" Nadie se mueve, así finalmente, en una voz muy simpática, Simón dice, "Abran los ojos y párense." y lo hacemos.

Hoy es una tarde muy rara. Los policía nos dan ejercicios muy extraños. Por ejemplo, Fernando dice "Marchen en el círculo.." Silvana dice, "Anden como gorilas." Luego Simón dice, "Caminen de puntillas en un círculo. Simón dice, " Caminen como elefantes." Luego Simón dice "Dígan 'Cuac, cuac, cuac' como un pato." "Dígan, 'Miau miau' como un gato," dice Silvana, pero nadie le pone atención. "Traten de volar como un pájaro" dice Fernando. Simón cree que esto es una buena idea. Simón repite, "Traten de volar como pájaros" pero no lo oímos. Simón dice, "Traten de volar como pájaros." Lo hacemos. Simón se ríe mucho. Simón dice, "¡Alto!"

Ahora es muy tarde. Simón pregunta, "¿Les gusta la fiesta?" Nadie dice nada. Simón dice, "Díganme que 'Sí!'" Nosotros gritamos, "¡Sí!" Fernando grita, "¡Anden a sus casas!" pero no nos vamos. Silvana grita, "¡Anden a sus casas!" pero no nos vamos. Simón grita, "¡Anden a sus casas!" pero no nos vamos.   Finalmente, en una voz muy simpática, Simón dice, "¡Anden a sus casas!" Y nos vamos.

NOTES:
* The plural commands are used in this story. You may want to simplify them to familiar singular commands.
* The commands that the students should respond to are underlined.

12. Voy, vas, va, vamos, van

Blues Style

Words and music by Patti Lozano

Melody A (Conjugation Ostinato*):

"Voy, vas, va, va - mos, van," Yo di-go, "Voy, vas, va, va-mos, van"Yo di-go,

"Voy, vas, va, va - mos, van" Voy, vas, va, va-mos van Ter-mi

- na-mos con "ir" y em-pe - za-mos con "po-der".

Melody B (Phrases):

Voy a... voy a pa-ti-nar. Vas a... vas a pa-ti-nar

Él va... Va a pa-ti-nar No-so-tros va-mos y

E -llos van en e -ne-ro, fe-bre-ro, mar-zo y a-bril

(clarinet interlude...)

(clarinet interlude)

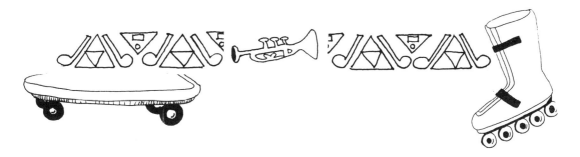

12.   Voy, vas, va, vamos van

Melody A:

Voy, vas, va, vamos, van
Yo digo: voy, vas, va, vamos, van
Yo digo: voy, vas, va, vamos, van
Voy, vas, va, vamos, van
Terminamos con "ir, "
Y empezamos con "poder"

Melody A:

I go, you go, he/she goes, we go, they /you [pl.] go
I say: I go, you go, he/she goes, we go, they/you [pl.] go
I say: I go, you go, he/she goes, we go, they/you [pl.] go
I go, you go, he/she goes, we go, they /you [pl.] go
We finish with "to go"
And we begin with "to be able to"

Melody B:

1. Voy a*...   voy a patinar*
   Vas a...   vas a patinar
   Él va...   va a patinar
   Nosotros vamos y
   Ellos van
   En enero, febrero, marzo y abril

2. Puedo, puedo patinar
   Puedes, puedes patinar
   Puede, él puede patinar
   Nosotros podemos y ellos pueden
   En mayo, junio, julio y agosto

3. Yo sé... Yo sé patinar...
   Tú sabes, tú sabes patinar
   Sabe, él sabe patinar
   Nosotros sabemos y ellos saben
   En septiembre, octubre,
        noviembre y diciembre

4. Vengo... vengo a patinar
   [vienes, viene, venimos, vienen]
   En el verano, el otoño,
        el invierno y la primavera

5. Salgo... salgo a patinar
   [sales, sale, salimos, salen] *(Fade out)*

Melody B;

1. *I'm going, I'm going to skate*
   You're going... etc
   He's going... etc.
   We're going
   They're going
   In January, February, March and April

2. *I can, I can skate*
   You can, you can skate
   He can, he can skate
   We can and they can
   In May, June, July and August

3. *I know how to skate*
   You know, you know how to skate
   He knows, he knows how to skate
   We know and they know
   In September, October,
        November and December

4. *I come to skate..*

   In the summer, the fall,
        the winter and spring

5. *I leave (go out)... I leave (go out) to skate*

♪ Notes ♪

* *"Ir a* + infinitive" means "going to ___". It is a simple way of talking about the future:
    Yo voy a escribir una carta. *(I'm going to write a letter.)*
    Ellos van a salir temprano. *(They're going to leave early.)*
* *"Patinar"* not only means "to skate". It also includes rollerblading and skateboarding.

12b

12. Voy, vas va, vamos, van

Grammar Objectives: ➤ Conjugation and use of irregular and stem-changing vebs

---

This song is interactive!
"**Voy, vas, va, vamos, van**" is a singin'-the-blues partner song. Although its original purpose is to drill stem-changing and irregular verbs, the same melodies and format can be used to practice any and all verbs and/or tenses.

    A. Melody A is a "conjugation ostinato". In music, an "ostinato" is defined as a melodic fragment that repeats continuously. Our Spanish students will continuously repeat conjugation drills instead of melodic fragments. Half of the students will sing verb conjugations while the other half sings the verses.

    B. Melody B is a verse that uses the verb being conjugated in a sentence. The verses all emphasize the *yo, tú, él, nosotros* and *ellos* structures. Both melodies are very simple; sing them together and you have great harmony and a very effective drill!

Grammar sprinkles
    A. Sing the verbs in other tenses.

        Examples: (future tense: *tener*)

            Melody A: *Tendré, tendrás, tendrá... etc.*

            Melody B: *Yo tendré.. Tendré nuevas patinas... etc.*

        (past tense: *querer*)

            Melody A: *Quise, quisiste, quiso... etc.*

            Melody B: *Yo quise... quise patinar... etc.*

    B. Exchange "*patinar*" for many other action verbs, *i.e. trabajar, correr, estornudar, platicar, rasgar,* etc.

Try this!
    A. Devise new groups of words to take the place of "*en enero, febrero, marzo y abril*" and subsequent groups of words (they are there more for rhythm and syncopation than any pedagogical purpose). You might suggest:

        * *places one skates: en la calle, en el camino, en la banqueta y el pavimento*

        * *skating weather: cuando hace frío, hace viento, hace calor o hace fresco*

        * *skating with people: con mi tío, mi amigo, mi abuelo y mi hermano*

    B. Devise a sequence of verbs that will help tell about an activity. Write them on "steps" as shown below, and sing from the bottom step up. Let's use the verb "*dibujar*" for this example, *i.e.* "*Aprendo a... aprendo a dibujar...etc.*"

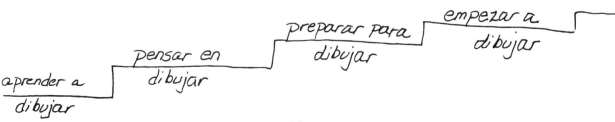

12. Voy, vas, va, vamos van

Melody A:

Voy, vas, va,   vamos, van
Yo digo: voy, vas, va,   vamos, van
Yo digo: voy, vas, va,   vamos, van
Voy, vas, va,   vamos, van
Terminamos con "ir " y empezamos con "poder"

Melody B:

VOY A, VAS A, VA A, VAMOS A, VAN A

1. Voy a...   voy a patinar
   Vas a...   vas a patinar
   Él va...   va a patinar
   Nosotros vamos y
   Ellos van   en enero, febrero, marzo y abril

2. Puedo, puedo patinar
   Puedes, puedes patinar
   Puede, él puede patinar
   Nosotros podemos y ellos pueden en mayo, junio, julio y agosto

   PUEDO, PUEDES, PUEDE, PODEMOS, PUEDEN

3. Yo sé... Yo sé patinar...
   Tú sabes, tú sabes patinar
   Sabe, él sabe patinar
   Nosotros sabemos y ellos saben en septiembre, octubre,
       noviembre y diciembre

   SE, SABES, SABE, SABEMOS, SABEN

4. Vengo... vengo a patinar
   Vienes... vienes a patinar
   Viene... él viene a patinar
   Nosotros venimos y ellos vienen en el verano, el otoño,
       el invierno y la primavera

   VENGO, VIENES, VIENE VENIMOS, VIENEN

5. Salgo... salgo a patinar
   Sales... sales a patinar
   Sale... él sale a patinar
   Nosotros salimos y ellos salen *(Fade out)*

   SALGO, SALES, SALE, SALIMOS, SALEN

13. Tú me regalaste un pastel ayer

Words and music by Patti Lozano

50's Style

Tú me re-ga-las-te un pas-tel a-yer. Me pro-me-tis-te u-na gran sor-pre-sa.

Tú me re-ga-las-te un pas-tel a-yer. Lo de-jas-te en a-que-lla me-sa. ¡Qué tri-

te-za sien-to hoy dí-a! Es la ver-dad que me quie-ro mo-rir. Cuan-do

fui-mos al jar-dín ¡mi pe-rro se lo co-mió! ¡Ay, no! Mi pe-rro

se lo co-mió, ¿Qué voy a ha cer? ¡Ay, no! Mi pe-rro se lo co-mió. ¡Ay de

mí! ¡Ay, no! Mi pe-rro se lo co-mió!

Estribillo:

1. D⁷

2. D   D⁷

(Instrumental)

13a

13. Tú me regalaste un pastel ayer

Tú me regalaste un pastel ayer
Me prometiste una gran sorpresa
Tú me regalaste un pastel ayer
Lo dejaste en aquella mesa.

Estribillo:
¡Qué tristeza siento hoy día!*
Es la verdad que me quiero morir
Cuando fuimos al jardín
Mi perro se lo comió
¡Ay, no! Mi perro se lo comió.
　　　　¿Qué voy a hacer?
¡Ay, no! Mi perro se lo comió.
　　　　¡Ay de mí! (2X)

2. Tú me regalaste un pastel ayer*
　　Te agradecí con un gran abrazo
　　Tú me regalaste un pastel ayer
　　No probé ni un sólo pedazo

3. Tú me regalaste un pastel ayer
　　De chocolate, porque es mi favorito
　　Tú me regalaste un pastel ayer
　　¡Qué mala suerte que le gusta mi perrito!

4. Tú me regalaste un pastel ayer
　　Con un corazón en azúcar amarillo
　　Tú me regalaste un pastel ayer
　　Y adentro escondiste un anillo

5. ¿Cómo voy a decírtelo
　　Que se tragó el pastel entero?
　　Tal vez yo te puedo regalar mi perro;
　　Porque ahora vale mucho dinero

Spoken during Fade out:　Ay, nunca me vas a
perdonar. ¿Porque tuve que comprar ese
perro? Mañana compraré un gato mejor.
¿Por qué metiste el anillo allí, mi amor?

You gave me a cake yesterday
You promised me a big surprise
You gave me a cake yesterday
You left it on that table

Refrain:
What sadness I feel today!
Truly I want to die
When we went to the garden
My dog ate it up.
Oh no! My dog ate it up!
　　　　What am I going to do?
Oh no! My dog ate it up!
　　　　Woe is me! (2X)

2. *You gave me a cake yesterday*
　　I thanked you with a big embrace
　　You gave me a cake yesterday
　　I didn't get to try a single piece

3. *You gave me a cake yesterday*
　　Of chocolate, because it's my favorite
　　You gave me a cake yesterday
　　What bad luck that my dog likes it too.

4. *You gave me a cake yesterday*
　　With a heart in yellow sugar
　　You gave me a cake yesterday
　　And inside you hid a ring

5. *How am I going to tell you*
　　That he swallowed the entire cake?
　　Maybe I can give you my dog
　　Because now he's worth a lot of money

Oh, you're never going to forgive me.
Why did I have to buy this dog?
Tomorrow I'm buying a cat. Why did
You hide the ring there, mi love?

♪ Notes ♪

　　* The descant (high second voice) heard behind "¡Que tristeza...etc." is "Lágrimas para mí hoy día, lágrimas y yo quiero morirme" (*translation. "Tears for me today, tears and I want to die"*)
　　* Don't forget the obligatory 50's claps on verses #2 and 4!

13. Tú me regalaste un pastel ayer

> **Grammar Objectives:** ➤ verbs, preterite tense

This song is interactive!

"**Tú me regalaste un pastel ayer**" is an affectionate parody of the innocent rock 'n roll songs of the late '50s and early '60s. The interactive activities stem from making use of every cliché common to pop songs of that era:

A. Add the traditional 50's claps (you can hear them in the recording on verses 2 and 4. The clapping rhythm is:

B. Add nonsensical ostinatos. (Remember from the previous song, "**Voy, vas, va, vamos, van**," an ostinato is a continuously repeating verbal or melodic fragment!) Your ostinato in this song can range from simple "*ooh waaah*" syllables to more complex "*Scooby, dooby, sha na nippy nu na*". The very best ostinato for instructional purposes is one that has relevance to the the story: brainstorm with the students to create an ostinato pattern to accompany each verse. For example, verse #3 centers around chocolate. Half of the class can sing the lyrics while the others chant or sing this ostinato phrase:

> "*Cho cho cho, me gusta chocolate, Dame*
> *Cho cho cho, me gusta chocolate*" (2X)

C. Have a student speak – not sing – one of the verses (verse #4 is a good one for this). Be sure to use a lot of tremulous emotion.

D. The refrain begs for choreography! Try these movements:

¡Ay, no!	*Mi perro*		*se lo comió.*
clap hands to cheeks	make "dog ears" on head with cupped hands		pantomime eating or rub stomach
¿Qué	*voy*	*a hacer?*	
	slap thighs	universal "What?" hand position (arms bent, palms facing up)	
¡Ay, no!	*Mi perro*	*se lo comió.*	
clap hands to cheeks	make "dog ears" on head with cupped hands	pantomime eating or rub stomach	
¡Ay de mí! (2X)			
universal "woe is me" stance (wrist tragically on forehead)			

Grammar sprinkles

To exercise conversing in the past tense play "**Whose Past?**"

A. Preparation: each student needs a pencil and an index card

B. Ask every student to write down five sentences on the index cards about his or her past. The past can have occured as recently as breakfast or the previous class period, for example:

> *"Comí huevos y pan tostado para mi desayuno."*

Or it can be about last week:

> *"Melinda y yo fuimos al cine con Miguel."*
>
> *"Mi reporte ganó un premio en la clase de ciencias."*

Or it can be about a childhood experience or milestone:

> *"Yo empecé a jugar al ténis en junio 1990."*
>
> *"En el segundo grado perdí un diente en el gimnasio."*

C. Gather and shuffle the cards. Redistribute them so that every student has a card other than his own.

D. Give each student a turn to read the five "past" sentences on his card after which the class tries to identify the person with that unique history.

 Try this!

A. Play "**Secret Rules**," a humorous group question and answer game that needs no materials or preparation!

1) Send one volunteer out of the room. While waiting outside, the student plans some past tense questions to ask classmates upon re-entering.

2) Meanwhile, the rest of the class chooses a secret rule to be followed when answering questions. Some ideas:

* *All answers begin with the word, "Pues..."*
* *All students must answer in the voices of grandparents.*
* *Students must clear throats at some point during the answer.*
* *Every answer must contain the word "rojo".*
* *All answers must be lies.*
* *All answers must be negative.*
* *Every answer must contain a number.*
* *Students must rub a body part during the answer.*

3) The student returns to the room. As he asks questions to various classmates and listens to answers, he must determine and identify the "secret rule"!

B. Write either a phrase from the song, or any preterite sentence on the board. Students take turns going to the board, erasing a word and substituting a new word. Sometimes, for grammatical accuracy, two or three words must be erased and added. Students may also add a word without erasing any. Each time the class reads the new sentence out loud.

> *Example:*
> * *Tú me regalaste un pastel ayer.*
> * *Tú me diste un pastel ayer.*
> * *Tú me diste una rana ayer.*
> * *Yo te di una rana ayer.*
> * *Yo te di una rana hoy.*
> * *Yo te di una rana apestosa hoy.*

13. Tú me regalaste un pastel ayer

Tú me regalaste un pastel ayer
Me prometiste una gran sorpresa
Tú me regalaste un pastel ayer
Lo dejaste en aquella mesa.

Estribillo:

¡Qué tristeza siento hoy día!
Es la verdad que me quiero morir
Cuando fuimos al jardín
Mi perro se lo comió
¡Ay, no! Mi perro se lo comió.
       ¿Qué voy a hacer?
¡Ay, no! Mi perro se lo comió.
       ¡Ay de mí! (2X)

2. Tú me regalaste un pastel ayer
   Te agradecí con un gran abrazo
   Tú me regalaste un pastel ayer
   No probé ni un sólo pedazo

3. Tú me regalaste un pastel ayer
   De chocolate, porque es mi favorito
   Tú me regalaste un pastel ayer
   ¡Qué mala suerte que le gusta mi perrito!

4. Tú me regalaste un pastel ayer
   Con un corazón en azúcar amarillo
   Tú me regalaste un pastel ayer
   Y adentro escondiste un anillo

5. ¿Cómo voy a decírtelo
   Que se tragó el pastel entero?
   Tal vez yo te puedo regalar mi perro;
   Porque ahora vale mucho dinero

14. En el pueblo

Words and music by Patti Lozano

A cumulative,
echo song

En el pue - blo (echo) hay u - na ca - lle, (echo) Hay u - na
2. pue - blo (echo) hay u - na ca - sa (echo) Hay u - na

ca - lle (echo) ¡Na - da más! (echo) ¿A la de - re - cha? U - na fle - cha. ¿A la iz
ca - sa (echo) ¡Na - da más! (echo)

spoken (Q & A):

-quier - da? U - na cuer - da. ¿Pa - ra a - trás? ¡Ra - tas, qui - zás! ¿Se -

gui - mos a - de - lan - te? ¡Ab - so - lu - ta - men - te!

1.

Al

2.

fon - do de la ca - lle... (echo) En el

Y a -

3. **Add an additional prepositional phrase to each repeated verse!**

den - tro de la ca - sa, (echo) al fon - do de la ca - lle... (echo)

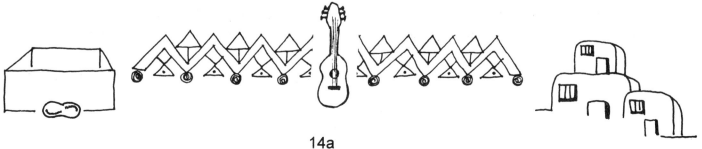

14. En el pueblo

En el pueblo (echo) hay una calle (echo)
Hay una calle (echo) nada más (echo)

Estribillo:
¿A la derecha? Una flecha.
¿A la izquierda? Una cuerda.
¿Para atrás? ¡Ratas quizás!
¿Seguimos adelante? ¡Absolutamente!

2. Al fondo de la calle
   En el pueblo hay una casa
   Hay una casa nada más

3. Y adentro de la casa, al fondo de la calle
   En el pueblo hay un sala
   Hay una sala nada más

4. And cerca de la sala, adentro de la casa,
      al fondo de la calle
   En el pueblo hay escaleras
   Hay escaleras nada más

5. Junto a las escaleras, cerca de la sala,
      adentro de la casa, al fondo de la calle
   En el pueblo hay un cuarto
   Hay un cuarto nada más

6. Y en medio del cuarto, junto a las escaleras
      cerca de la sala, adentro de la casa,
      al fondo de la calle
   En el pueblo hay una cama... etc.

7. Y debajo de la cama, en medio del cuarto,
      junto a las escaleras, cerca de la sala
      adentro de la casa, al fondo de la calle
   En el pueblo hay una caja... etc.

8. Y delante de la caja, debajo de la cama... etc.
   En el pueblo hay un cacahuate
   Hay un cacahuate, ¡Y me lo comí!

In the village (echo) there's a street (echo)
There's a street (echo) nothing else (echo)

Refrain:
To the right? An arrow
To the left? A rope
Behind? Rats, perhaps!
Do we continue on ahead? Absolutely!

2. At the end o the street
   In the village there's a house
   There's a house nothing else

3. And inside the house, at the end of the street
   In the village there's a living room
   There's a living room nothing else

4. And near the living room, inside the house,
      at the end of the street
   In the village there's a staircase
   There's a staircase nothing else

5. Close to the stairs, near the living room,
      inside the house, at the end of the street
   In the village there's a room
   There's a room nothing else

6. And in the middle of the room, close to
      the stairs, near the living room, inside
      the house, at the end of the street
   In the village There's a bed... etc.

7. And under the bed, in the middle of the room...
      close to the stairs, near the living room
      inside the house, at the end of the street
   In the village There's a box... etc.

8. And in front of the box, under the bed... etc.
   In the village There's a peanut....
   There's a peanut.... and I ate it!

♪ **Notes** ♪ Refrain #4: alacranes *(scorpions)* #5: cucarachas *(cochroaches)* #6: arañas *(spiders)*

14. En el pueblo

| Grammar Objectives: | ➤ prepositions and prepositional phrases |

 This song is interactive!

"En el pueblo" brings to mind such interactive campfire songs as *"The Green Grass Grows All Around"* and *"Sippin' Cider,"* although this one is a bit spooky and consistently spotlights prepositional phrases. Try these ideas:

A. As you can hear in the recording, **En el pueblo** is a an "echo" song. Either you, a student, or a small group of students sing the lead phrases. Everyone sings the echo.

B. **"En el pueblo"** is a cumulative song. An additional prepositional phrase is added in each verse. Make a transparency of the song map on page **14e** to keep your place in the song!

C. Devise choreography for the chanted refrain.

 Grammar sprinkles

A. Concentrate on the street, the house and yard, or a room in the house. Enlarge the illustration on page **14e** or draw a likeness on the board. No longer is there *"una cama - nada más"* because the students are going to draw and describe more features, for example:

　　* *En lo alto de las escaleras hay una planta.*
　　* *Al lado izquierdo de la calle hay un buzón azul.*
　　* *Encima del techo hay una chimenea.*
　　* *Detrás de la cama hay cortinas muy finas.*

B. Create a unique class song with all new verses titled "En el centro".

 Try this!

A. Notice that during several refrains in the recording, the high school singers improvised upon frightful creatures to avoid. Choose a different volunteer to solo and state his own terrifying creature in each refrain.

B. Play **"Fruit Roll"**.

　1) Preparation: Each student needs a sturdy round or almost-round fruit, such as an orange, grapefruit, cantaloupe, apple, lemon or lime. If you want to blend the song into this activity, set up a cardboard house and a construction paper street on the floor in front of it. (Don't forget to set up a cardboard rat!)

　2) Game: Each student gets a turn to state his intent with his piece of fruit and then to execute a "fruit roll". Students that achieve their goals receive a point. Goals might be:

　　* *Voy a poner mi naranja en frente de la casa.*
　　* *Voy a poner mi naranja al lado derecho de la casa.*
　　* *Voy a poner mi toronja entre las dos naranjas.*
　　* *Voy a poner mi limón en medio de la calle.*

　　Students whose fruit knocks down the cardboard rat have to perform a "forfeit" (consult the forfeit page in the back of the book).

14. En el pueblo

En el pueblo *(echo)* hay una calle *(echo)*
Hay una calle *(echo)*   nada más *(echo)*

Estribillo:
¿A la derecha?   Una flecha.
¿A la izquierda?   Una cuerda.
¿Para atrás?   ¡Ratas quizás!
¿Seguimos adelante?   ¡Absolutamente!

2. Al fondo de la calle
   En el pueblo   hay una casa
   Hay una casa   nada más

3. Y adentro de la casa, al fondo de la calle
   En el pueblo hay un sala
   Hay una sala   nada más

4. And cerca de la sala, adentro de la casa, al fondo de la calle
   En el pueblo hay escaleras
   Hay escaleras   nada más

5. Junto a las escaleras, cerca de la sala,
      adentro de la casa, al fondo de la calle
   En el pueblo   hay un cuarto
   Hay un cuarto   nada más

6. Y en medio del cuarto, junto a las escaleras
      cerca de la sala, adentro de la casa, al fondo de la calle
   En el pueblo   hay una cama
   Hay una cama   nada más

7. Y debajo de la cama, en medio del cuarto,
      junto a las escaleras, cerca de la sala
      adentro de la casa, al fondo de la calle
   En el pueblo   hay una caja
   Hay una caja   nada más

8. Y delante de la caja, debajo de la cama, en medio del cuarto,
   junto a las escaleras, cerca de la sala, adentro de la casa, al fondo de la calle
   En el pueblo   hay un cacahuate
   Hay un cacahuate, ¡Y me lo comí!

14. En el pueblo

15. La Palapa

Words and music by Patti Lozano

Tropical

Co- ra ca- mi- na- ba en la pla- ya a- quel dí - a, ca- mi - na- ba en la a- re- na al
un can- gre- jo en el ta- lón del pie Y Co- ra se pu- so a sal-

la- do del mar. Co- ra no pen- sa- ba en na - da,
tar. Gri -tó, "¡A- yú- de- me al - guien! ¡No quie- ro mo- rir -me!

Só- lo que- rí- a an - dar, cuan- do le pi- có
¡Al- go me quie - re a - ta- car!" Y co- rrió ha- cia "La Pa - la- pa," fa- mo- sa en la

pla- ya de Ix- ta- pa, Sus pal- me- ras, sus nie- ves de san- dí- a y li- món. "La Pa -

la- pa," fa- mo- sa en la pla- ya de Ix- ta- pa, En tu men- te y en tu co- ra-

zón, Sí, sí, siem- pre en tu men- te y en tu co- ra - zón

15. "La Palapa"

Cora caminaba en la playa aquel día
Caminaba en la arena al lado del mar
Cora no pensaba en nada
Sólo quería andar   cuando le picó

Cora walked on the beach that day
She walked in the sand by the side of the sea
Cora wasn't thinking of anything
She just wanted to walk

Un cangrejo en el talón del pie
Y Cora se puso a saltar
Gritó, "¡Ayúdeme alguien! ¡No quiero morirme!
¡Algo me quiere atacar!" Y corrió hacia

When a crab bit her on the heel of her foot
And Cora began to jump around
She screamed, "Help me someone, I don't want to die!
Something wants to attack me!" And she ran toward

Estribillo:
La Palapa*, famosa en la playa de Ixtapa,
Sus palmeras, sus nieves de sandía y limón
La Palapa,   famosa en la playa de Ixtapa,
En tu mente y en tu corazón
Sí, sí, siempre en tu mente y en tu corazón
Sí, sí, siempre en tu mente y en tu corazón

Refrain:
La Palapa, famous on the Ixtapa beach
It's palm trees, it's watermelon and lemon ices
La Palapa, famous on the Ixtapa beach
Always in your mind and heart
Yes, yes, always in your mind and heart
Yes, yes, always in your mind and heart

2. Enrique estaba trabajando en La Palapa
   Cuando oyó los chillidos de terror
   Corrió por la puerta, su mente alerta
   Para buscar ese grito de dolor   Y vió que

Enrique was working at La Palapa
When he heard the shrieks of terror
He ran to the door, his mind alert
To search for this cry of pain. And he saw that

   Cora estaba sentada en la arena
   Agarrándose el pie y a punto de llorar
   Enrique se bajó y a Cora miró
   Y en seguida la empezó a abrazar
      en frente de

3. Cora was sitting in the sand
Holding her foot and on the verge of crying
Enrique bent down and looked at Cora
And tenderly he began to hug her
in front of

Estribillo

Refrain

3. Cora volvió a Chicago (es abogada)
   Enrique volvió a trabajar
   En momentos flojos Cora cierra los ojos
   Y luego empieza a soñar de

4. Cora returned to Chicago (she's a lawyer)
Enrique returned to his work
In lazy moments Cora closes her eyes
And then she begins to daydream of

Estribillo

Refrain

♪ Notes ♪

   "*Palapa*" is the name for thatched roofs made out of palm fronds, found in many tropical locations. In this song, "*La Palapa*" is also the name of a little restaurant on the beach.

15. La Palapa

Grammar Objectives: ➢ verbs; the preterite vs. the imperfect tense

This song is interactive!

"**La Palapa**" is a ballad, and like the other earlier ballads in this collection ("Estoy andando, estoy buscando" and "Tú me regalaste un pastel ayer",) once the class is familiar with the song, two students may act out the story as the class sings it.

Grammar sprinkles

A. Create some comments, questions and exclamations for a group of back-up singers, who will insert these short remarks at the end of sung phrases. Here is an example with the back-up singers' quips underlined:

> *Cora caminaba en la playa aquel día*
> *Caminaba en la arena al lado del mar ¿En qué pensaba?*
> *Cora no pensaba en nada   No trabajaba*
> *Sólo quería andar ¿Y qué pasó?   cuando le picó*

B. News Flash! Turn Cora's tropical vacation into a newsworthy story. Create a flashy headline, (*i.e.* "*Cangrejo Ataca a Turista en Ixtapa*") and follow it with a lurid, detailed description of events. Here is an example:

> *"A las 3:20 de la tarde del 12 de agosto,*
> *Cora Valenzuela, una joven abogada de Chicago,*
> *caminaba en la playa de Ixtapa. Cora estaba*
> *sola, sus compañeras descansaban en el hotel.*
> *Según Cora, "Yo no pensaba en nada. Sólo*
> *quería andar." Aparentemente a Cora le gusta*
> *mucho caminar en la playa todas las tardes.*
> *Pero esa tarde fue diferente..."*

Try this!

A. Ixtapa is a lovely resort town on the Pacific coast of southern Mexico. The map on page **15e** shows the location of many Mexican vacation spots.

1) Research the tourist towns on the map. Write a sentence about each one:

> *Examples: ¡Hace treinta años el pueblo de Ixtapa no existía!*
> *La isla de Cozumel es famosa por el coral negro.*
> *Acapulco es la capital del estado de Guerrero.*

2) Have each student compose a catchy two-line poem about one or more popular beach resort/towns. Compile them to have a class poem.

> *Example: A los Americanos les encanta Cancún*
> *Cerca hay una ruina que se llama Tulúm*

The poem does not have to make sense!

> *Example: Zihuatanejo, yo te dejo*
> *Cuida mucho a mi conejo*

B. To reinforce and practice both new and review vocabulary, play "**Bag of Words**"
   1) Preparation: Make a list of the words you want to drill. Write each word on a slip of paper, fold it, and place all of them into a bag. If your lesson focuses on a particular verb tense, be sure to indicate it on the paper. Have another bag with slips of paper containing all of the students' names.
   2) Activity: Have each student pull seven words out of the word bag, and one student's name out of the name bag. They must each write a short story (no more than three paragraphs) that uses every word they picked out at least one time. The protagonist of the story is the name pulled out of the name bag.

C. For a totally improvisational activity that highlights usage of past and preterite tenses, play "**¡Ay, qué bueno! No, ¡es malo!**" You can also play this activity in present tense.
   1) Preparation: none
   2) Make a simple statement to the class.
      Example: Eran las vacaciones y Marcos estaba en su casa.
   3) The whole class exclaims enthusiastically, "*¡Ay qué bueno!*"
   4) Student A says, "*No, es malo*" and proceeds to explain why.
      Example: Marcos estaba muy aburrido.
   5) The whole class exclaims with dismay, "*¡Ay, qué malo!*"
   6) Student B disagrees, saying, "*No, es bueno*" and explains why.
      Example: Marcos estaba aburrido y por eso decidió ir
      a la alberca.
   7) Who knows what path this story will follow? The only thing certain is that it will become sillier and sillier!
      Example: Class: ¡Ay, qué bueno!
      Student C: No, es malo. Marcos caminó sin zapatos y se
      cortó el pie.
      Class: ¡Ay, qué malo!
      Student D: No, es bueno. Una muchacha bonita lo llevó
      en su motocicleta.
      Class: ¡Ay, qué bueno!
      Student E: No, es malo. Marcos y la muchacha se
      perdieron...

15. "La Palapa"

Versos
Cora caminaba en la playa aquel día
Caminaba en la arena al lado del mar
Cora no pensaba en nada
Sólo quería andar   cuando le picó

Un cangrejo en el talón del pie
Y Cora se puso a saltar
Gritó, "¡Ayúdeme alguien! ¡No quiero morirme!
¡Algo me quiere atacar!" Y corrió hacia

Estribillo:
La Palapa, famosa en la playa de Ixtapa,
Sus palmeras, sus nieves de sandía y limón
La Palapa,   famosa en la playa de Ixtapa,
En tu mente y en tu corazón
Sí, sí, siempre en tu mente y en tu corazón
Sí, sí, siempre en tu mente y en tu corazón
Sí, sí, siempre en tu mente y en tu corazón

2. Enrique estaba trabajando en La Palapa
   Cuando oyó los chillidos de terror
   Corrió por la puerta, su mente alerta
   Para buscar ese grito de dolor   Y vió que

   Cora estaba sentada en la arena
   Agarrándose el pie y a punto de llorar
   Enrique se bajó y a Cora miró
   Y en seguida la empezó a abrazar
      en frente de

3. Cora volvió a Chicago (es abogada)
   Enrique volvió a trabajar
   En momentos flojos Cora cierra los ojos
   Y luego empieza a soñar de

15. La Palapa

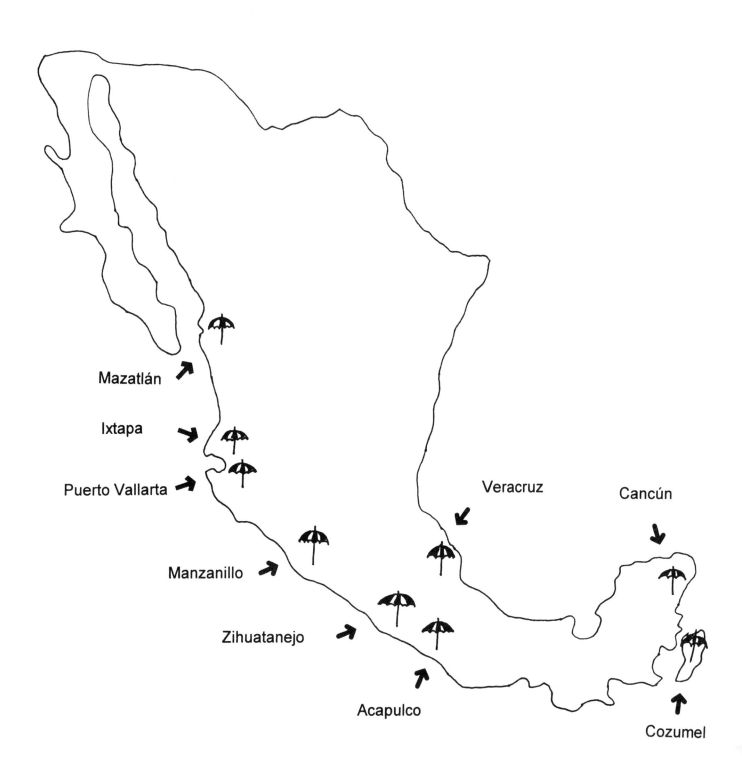

Mazatlán

Ixtapa

Puerto Vallarta

Manzanillo

Zihuatanejo

Acapulco

Veracruz

Cancún

Cozumel

Appendix

Vocabulary Guide to "e" Page Illustrations

1e: el lápiz   el cuaderno
     el libro   el bolígrafo
     la regla   las tijeras
     el legajo   la calculadora

1f: los lápices   los cuadernos
     los libros   los bolígrafos
     las reglas   las tijeras
     los legajos   las calculadoras

("*el legajo*" is also known as "*la carpeta*")

2e: The first two illustrations are adults and should be addressed as "*usted.*"

Countries: México   *   el Perú   *   El Salvador
           España *Spain*   Ecuador   *   la Argentina

3e: tímido(a)   *shy*   romántico(a) *romantic*   cínico(a)   *cynical*
     simpático(a) *nice*   cansado(a)   *tired*   alegre   *happy*
     triste   *sad*   enojado(a)   *angry*   aburrido(a)   *bored*
     bobo(a)   *foolish*   loco(a)   *crazy*   preocupado(a) *worried*

4e   grande *big*   mediano(a) *medium*   pequeño(a) *small*   feo(a) *ugly*
     bonito(a) *pretty* interesante *interesting* inteligente *intelligent* calmado(a) *calm*
     nervioso(a) *nervous* popular *popular*   gordo(a) *fat*   delgado *skinny*
     débil *weak*   musculoso *muscular*   extrovertido(a) *friendly* deprimido(a) *depressed*

5. caminar   *walk*   dibujar *draw*   escribir *write*   trabajar work
    bailar   *dance*   tocar   *play an instrument* jugar *play a sport*   limpiar *clean*
    escuchar *listen*   correr *run*   comer *eat*   leer *read*
    viajar   *travel* escribir *write*   cantar *sing*   subir *climb*

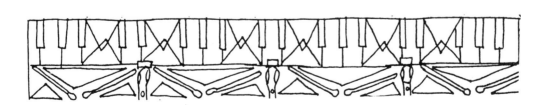

18

Forfeit Page

When students or teams answer questions correctly in games or activities you often award them a point or a treat. Occasionally when students get questions wrong in a game, you may want to have them perform a "forfeit". Here is a list of entertaining, but innocent forfeits.

✓ Say the twelve months in Spanish in reverse order (*diciembre* to *enero*)

✓ Untie and retie a classmate's shoes

✓ Perform an impersonation of Antonio Banderas

✓ Spell "*otorolongólogo*" (it's an ear, nose and throat specialist)!

✓ Compose a two-line poem with the rhyming words "*amigo*" and "*abrigo*"

✓ Name five words that end in "-*ción*"

✓ Declare your love to the person sitting to your right

✓ Make up a short song titled "Me gusta hablar español"

✓ Read a paragraph from your Spanish textbook and act it out

✓ Imitate a burro

✓ Sing "Happy Birthday" in the style of Ricky Martin

✓ Spell three classmate's names in Spanish

✓ Balance your textbook on your head (no hands) while counting to twenty in Spanish

✓ Crawl around the classroom floor while saying, "*¡Ven, mi conejito! ¡Vente a Papá!*"

✓ Name eleven colors in twenty seconds

✓ Name and touch ten classroom objects in twenty seconds.

✓ Grab two friends, join hands and circle around while singing the chorus to "Cielito Lindo" (the "*¡Ay, ay, ay, ay...!*" section)

✓ Balance a goldfish cracker on your nose while conjugating a verb (teacher's choice)

✓ Create a cheer in Spanish that incorporates the name of an animal

Guitar Chords and Transposition Charts

How to use these charts

If a song is written in the key of C, the chord progression probably includes some or all of the these chords: C, G, F, Dm, Am and Em.   You can play the song in another key (**"transpose"** the melody) by using a different set of guitar chords.   The language teacher's top two reasons for transposing a song to a new key are probably:

    1) to play the song in a higher or lower key which is easier for you and/or your students' voices to sing

    2) to play easier guitar chords

On the following page are guitar chord diagrams for all of the basic chords, including all of the chords used in **Spanish Grammar Swings!** To change to a new key, just use the chords that are in a different row.   Here is an example:

> You are looking at song #12 "**Voy,vas,va,vamos,van**", which is written in the key of C (no flats or sharps),and uses primarily the chords of C, F^7, G and G^7. You do not want to play F^7 because it is a "bar" chord and you're scared of bar chords. You consult the Guitar Chords and Transposition Chart and decide to change to the key to D where you can wow your students with D, G^7, A and A^7.

How to read a guitar chord diagram:

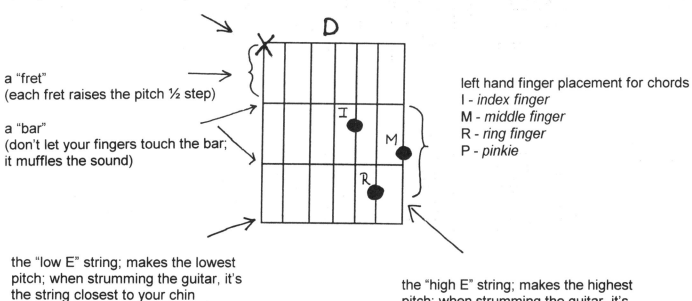

don't strum this string during this chord
(the pitch is not in the chord)

a "fret"
(each fret raises the pitch ½ step)

a "bar"
(don't let your fingers touch the bar;
it muffles the sound)

left hand finger placement for chords
I - *index finger*
M - *middle finger*
R - *ring finger*
P - *pinkie*

the "low E" string; makes the lowest pitch; when strumming the guitar, it's the string closest to your chin

the "high E" string; makes the highest pitch; when strumming the guitar, it's the string closest to your lap

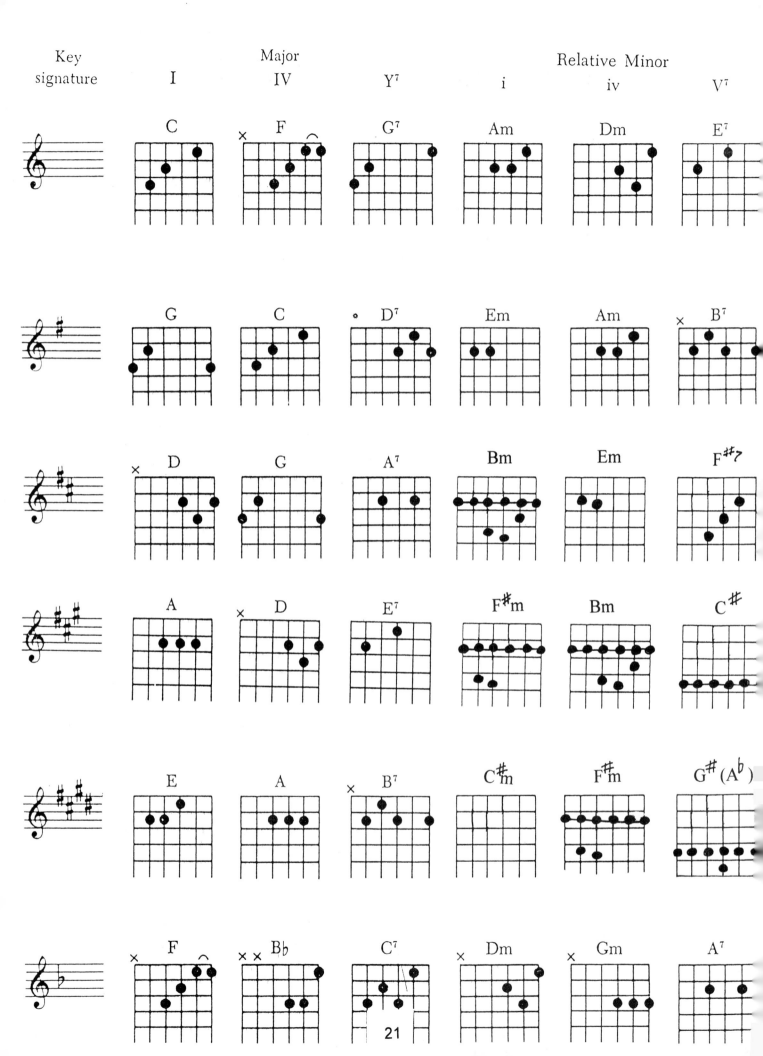

Bibliography

Campbell, Don. 1997. *The Mozart Effect.* New York: Avon Books

Cassady, Marsh. 1996. *Acting Games.* Colorado Springs, Colorado: Meriwether Publishing

Dickson, Heather. *50 of the Finest Adult Party Games*, 1999. LAGOON BOOKS, UK

Dickson, Heather. *50 of the Finest After Dinner Games*, 1999. LAGOON BOOKS, UK

Gardner, Howard. 1982. *Art, Mind and Brain: A Cognitive Approach to Creativity.* New York: Basic Books

Jensen, Eric. 2000. *Music with the Brain in Mind,* San Diego, CA. The Brain Store, Inc.

Gregson, Bob. 1982. *The Incredible Indoor Games Book.* Torrance, CA. Fearon Teacher Aids

Lozano, Patti. 1999. *Get Them Talking!* Houston, Tex: Dolo Publications

Murphey, Tim. 1992. *Music and Song.* Corby, England: Oxford University Press

Ur, Penny & Wright, Andrew. 1992. *Five-Minute Activities.* UK. Cambridge University Press

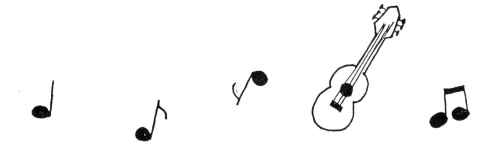

Information and Order Page

Dolo Publications, Inc
12800 Briar Forest Dr #23
Houston Texas 77077
e-mail: dolo@wt.net

Tel. (281) 493-4552 or
(281) 463-6694
Fax (281) 679-9092
Www.dololanguages.com

Send Check Charge, Fax or Purchase Order to above address, or
Cal Toll Free **1-800-830-1460** to place an order

ITEM	DESCRIPTION	UNIT PRICE	TOTAL
MS1	MUSIC THAT TEACHES SPANISH		
	BOOK AND CD*	$31.95	
MM2	MORE MUSIC THAT TEACHES SPANISH		
	BOOK AND CD*	$31.95	
ME5	MUSIC THAT TEACHES ENGLISH		
	BOOK AN CD*	$31.95	
MF7	MUSIC THAT TEACHES FRENCH		
	BOOK AND CD*	$31.95	
MG9	MUSIC THAT TEACHES GERMAN		
	BOOK AND CD	$31.95	
LC3	¡LEYENDAS CON CANCIONES!		
	BOOK AND CD* & ACTIVITY MASTER	$31.95	
SGS8	SPANISH GRAMMAR SWINGS!		
	BOOK AND CD*	$31.95	
TCH10	TEATRO DE CUENTOS DE HADAS	$24.95	
	MIGHTY MINI-PLAYS PRICE EACH PS4SPANISH_ _ _ PF4FRENCH_ _ _ PG4GERMAN_ _ _ PE4ELS_ _ _	$21.95	
GT6	GET THEM TALKING!	$21.95	
	SNLI/II SING 'N LEARN VERBS IN SPANISH OR II EA	$21.95	
JMCD	JUST MUSIC CD	$10.00	
BROOKS WITH * ALSO AVAILABLE WITH AUDIO-CASSETTE		$29.95	
	SUB-TOTAL		
	SHIPPING & HANDLING 10%, $4.00 MINIMUM		
	ADD 8.25% SALES TAX WHEN APPLICABLE		
	TOTAL		

Manner of Payment:
Check_____ Charge _____ Purchase Order #_____
Name _____
School _____ District: _____
Address: _____
City _____ State _____ Zip Code _____

Charge Card Information:
Cardholder Name _____
Street Address _____
City* State* Zip _____
Phone H: (   ) _____
Credit Card Number: (VISA or MasterCard Only)

Expiration Date ____/____/____ (include 3 Number on signature strip)
NOTE: School districts, please Purchase Order. Allow 2-3 weeks delivery.